Glare

Also by A. R. Ammons

Ommateum

Expressions of Sea Level

Corsons Inlet

Tape for the Turn of the Year

Northfield Poems

Selected Poems

Uplands

Briefings

Collected Poems: 1951–1971
(winner of the National Book Award for Poetry, 1973)

Sphere: The Form of a Motion
(winner of the 1973–1974 Bollingen Prize in Poetry)

Diversifications

The Snow Poems

Highgate Road

The Selected Poems: 1951–1977

Selected Longer Poems

A Coast of Trees
(winner of the National Book Critics Circle Award for Poetry, 1981)

Worldly Hopes

Lake Effect Country

The Selected Poems: Expanded Edition

Sumerian Vistas

The Really Short Poems

Garbage
(winner of the National Book Award for Poetry, 1993)

Brink Road

Glare

A. R. Ammons

W. W. Norton

& Company

New York

London

The first section of Part One first appeared in the *Paris Review*, 1996. The first seven sections of Part Two appeared in *Epoch*, 1997. I am grateful to the editors for permission to reprint these materials.

For information about permission to reproduce selections from this book, write to Permissions, W. W. Norton & Company, Inc., 500 Fifth Avenue, New York, NY 10110.

The text of this book is composed in 10.5 on 13.5 Janson
with the display set in Centaur Monotype Bold at 70% horizontal scale
Composition by PennSet, Inc.
Manufacturing by Courier Companies, Inc.

Library of Congress Cataloging-in-Publication Data
Ammons, A. R., 1926–
    Glare / by A. R. Ammons.
      p.   cm.
    ISBN 0-393-04096-8
    I. Title.
  PS3501.M6G53   1997
811'.54—dc21   96-48506
                          CIP

W. W. Norton & Company, Inc., 500 Fifth Avenue,
New York, N.Y. 10110
http://www.wwnorton.com

W. W. Norton & Company Ltd., 10 Coptic Street, London WC1A 1PU

1 2 3 4 5 6 7 8 9 0

With love to my grandson
Matthew Irving Ammons

Part One

Strip

wdn't it be silly to be serious, now:
I mean, the hardheads and the eggheads

are agreed that we are an absurd
irrelevance on this slice of curvature

and that a boulder from the blue
could confirm it: imagine, mathematics

wiped out by a wandering stone, or
grecian urns not forever fair when

the sun expands: can you imagine
cracking the story off we've built

up so long—the simian ancestries,
the lapses and leaps, the discovery

of life in the burial of grains:
the scratch of pictorial and syllabic

script, millennia of evenings around
the fires: nothing: meaninglessness

our only meaning: our deepest concerns
such as death or love or child-pain

arousing a belly laugh or a witty
dismissal: a bunch of baloney: it's

already starting to feel funny: I
think I may laugh: few of the dead

lie recalled, and they have not
cautioned us: we are rippers and

tearers and proceeders: restraint
stalls us still—we stand hands

empty, lip hung, dumb eyes struck
open: if we can't shove at the

trough, we don't understand: but is
it not careless to become too local

when there are four hundred billion
stars in our galaxy alone: at

least, that's what I heard: also,
that there are billions of such

systems spread about, some older,
some younger than ours: if the

elements are the elements thruout,
I daresay much remains to be learned:

however much we learn, tho, we may
grow daunted by our dismissibility

in so sizable a place: do our gods
penetrate those reaches, or do all

those other places have their godly
nativities: or if the greatest god

Strip

is the stillness all the motions add
up to, then we must ineluctably be

included: perhaps a dribble of
what-is is what what-is is: it is

nice to be included, especially from
so minor a pew: please turn, in yr

hymnals, to page "Archie carrying on
again": he will have it his way

though he has no clue what his way
is: after such participations as

that with the shrill owl in the
spruce at four in the morning with

the snow ended and the moon come
out, how am I sagely to depart from

all being (universe and all—by
that I mean material and immaterial

stuff) without calling out—just a
minute, am I not to know at last

what lies over the hill: over the
ridge there, over the laps of the

ocean, and out beyond the plasmas
of the sun's winds, and way out

where the bang still bubbles in the
longest risings: no, no: I must

get peanut butter and soda crackers
and the right shoe soles (for ice)

and leave something for my son and
leave these lines, poor things, to

you, if you will have them, can they
do you any good, my trade for my

harm in the world: come, let's
celebrate: it will all be over

where is one to find room enough to
write in: is the planet too small

now—for words: and having seen
into the instants of universal

beginning and knowing as we now know
the last seconds of the universal close

—are words drowned or drowned out or
still floating buoyantly tagging

this and that, splintering clogs,
warping bends into screw-you mood

stances: what are words to do, turn
to pictures, leave it to visuals,

oh, the spirit dies, but the body
lives forever, run out of its limits

though and caught up into others,
the housing spirits of others,

mold feed, ant freight, the mouth
parts and anuses of riddling larvae:

alas, not as ourselves do we come
again or go anywhere else, after we

go: oh, we go, we go, we go, so
long—forever: though, when we go,

Glare

it is only for an instant and then
we are gone, and staying gone, we

are gone timelessly and once and for
all: a quick trip covering eternity

so what is it to be while we are here
in this splendid (America) place:

must we be only splendid and, if not,
trash: can't we be young if not

eternally young, our muscles at the
peak, our body weight in grams, our

teeth even, bright, eternally brushed:
generations of bacteria arise in the

mouth that the next drink washes
away: and ages of fauna ride

out with the feces: microscopic mites
territorialize our faces, a species

for the eyelids, one for the cheek
bones, the nose, etc: I may be

making this up: am I someone who
just says things: would I say

anything to get it into play: do I
move the troops out onto opposite

blazes of the plain to know the
"field" of how they meet: will I give

my life to one side against the other
or will I side with neither but

stick around to praise the winner,
perhaps partake of the bubbly of

victory—not the loser's damp
ground and groans: or feel for

both, pain and joy that mean nothing,
my spirit unworthy of the sufferers

and the victors: is there no side
but one side or the other: can't

one observe and meditate: sometimes
in the last weeks of cancer when all

has been tried (and some of it close
to killing) and when life is seen

complete, nothing to be expected
and nothing expected of anyone, the

sick one's spirit shines and we
who don't yet know how sweet an hr

can be or how long another minute,
we don't know why: in extremis, is

love the main thing and the memory
of some other person diamonds,

rubies, sapphires, and emeralds

I keep proving I'm not god's gift to
the world by trying to prove I am:

is a big ego the shell of a rotten
egg: well, I think not: is a big

ego the size of the emptiness: not
what is full but what wants to fill:

whereas, doesn't the worthy person
excuse himself over and over, saying

until it makes your blood boil, I am
unworthy, anyone can do it: the web

we weave when we practice not to
deceive requires more training: with

a straight move, you can lie and
deceive: but to be honest you must

work off all the impurities, skim
the scum, strain out the niblets,

fine-tune the flame, before the simple
truth is simply said: it's so easy

to be crooked, no wonder so many
people head straight for it: I, trying (and

failing) to be honest, shrink from
easy identifications, such as being

a member of a movement or school or
kind of behavior: it seems it would

be so easy to be outrageous, yet it
must not be because so many look

worshipfully to that: no, no, no,
I say, and back off: no, no, I don't

want any of that: trying to be
honest, tho, is so colorless: it

has no flash or gimmick, no clear
category: it will get you million

and book contract nil: I haven't
even been called an environmentalist

yet: I've been called a nature poet
but that meant human nature, whatever

that is: ha, ha: wit from pain,
tears from joy, love from violence,

a cattybiarsoned world, oh, yeah:
oh, yeah

hear me, O Lord, from the height of
the high place, where speaking is not

necessary to hearing and hearing is
in all languages: hear me, please,

have mercy, for I have hurt people,
though I think not much and where

much never intentionally and I have
accumulated a memory (and some heavy

fantasy) guilt-ridden and as a
nonreligious person, I have no way

to assuage, relieve, or forgive
myself: I work and work to try to

redeem old wrong with present good:
but I'm not even sure my good is good

or who it's really for: I figure I
can be forgiven, nearly, at least,

by forgiving; that is, by understanding
that others, too, are caught up in

flurries of passion, of anger and
resentment and, my, my, jealousy and

that coincidences and unintentional
accidents of unwinding ways can't

be foreknown: what is started here,
say, cannot be told just where to

go and can't be halted midway and
can't, worst, be brought

back and started over: we are not,
O You, at the great height, whoever

you are or whatever, if anything, we
are not in charge, even though we

riddle localities with plans,
schemes, too, and devices, some of

them shameful or shameless: half-guilty
in most cases, sometimes in all, we

are half-guilty, and we live in
pain but may we suffer in your cool

presence, may we weep in your surround-
ing that already has understood:

we could not walk here without our
legs, and our feet kill, our

steps however careful: if you can
send no word silently healing, I

mean if it is not proper or realistic
to send word, actual lips saying

Strip

these broken sounds, why, may we be
allowed to suppose that we can work

this stuff out the best we can and
having felt out our sins to their

deepest definitions, may we walk with
you as along a line of trees, every

now and then your clarity and warmth
shattering across our shadowed way

seems like every winter the outside
chills a mouse inside and then there

you are: historical diseases and
funny viruses from Arizona: last

winter we thought we'd missed a
visitor, when my wife pulled up a

couch cushion, and there was a clutch
of nuts—walnuts (how his mouth

got around those who knows), pecans
and stuff off the breakfast table:

got him: last night as I relished
sitcoms, I noticed a flashback, a

mouse had appeared at a corner and
flashed away: so I searched up the

traps and cheese, and this morning
there he lay belly up with the trap

on top: he had got the wire not
across the head or neck but across

the middle and had probably leaped
and tossed some, clacking the trap

a foot or two away from center before
he lost the case: just when he

thought he had it made: when is
it ever more than a passing thought

in this life: I affirm nothing except
that I affirm nothing: just give me

breezes in the treezes and let wisdom
out the door: where I came from it

wouldn't be smart to talk about art:
talk about sawing logs or getting

the swamp hogs up or worming tobacco
or gutting ditches would be a lot

safer: when in Rome: don't try to
get the Romans to do what you do:

the highest place, though, is my idea
of the highest place and whose seat

it is (along with the seat) is my
projection, nothing more: and the

occupant, for all I know, may value
the lowest place more or assuming

an equatorial rondure may like one
pole as much as another; or, of

course, may not go in for valuation
of any kind: the lowest may be where

our Energy comes from, and the highest
may be a wilting out into pellucid

directionlessness: in other words,
I don't know what I'm talking about:

but if I understood my source as
from the depths (wherever) I might

think it silly to plead mercy (for
what) in all those fadings-away of

lofty subtleties: to have felt the
onset of a deep-energy source, to

cry out for one's own, to piss up
the landmarks of one's own place,

Strip

to fill women with food and seed,
to climb up any high place one can

find and sing (like a bird) I, I:
isn't this as good as withering away

on the upmost fringes of vanishing
self-excuse: there really is a

pecking order of peckers: measly
peckered guys feel like covering up

in showers, and swingers clunk about
like metronomes, a rhythm noted and

fiercely despised even by the moderate:
but the lugubriously weighty members,

they seem bestial and need to be
tied up: nevertheless, there may be

those who prefer them to the dinky
winks: the dabblers: the little

bitty bouncers, splintery, lacking heft
or duration of stroke: other

orders apply, though: and overcompensating
executives order regulars around,

mere laborers not at the crevice:
in life, I'll tell you, you have to

bend down and get what you can: you
may have to peck around the biscuit

when the biscuit's gone, drain a drop
of honey from a bottle already tossed:

git in there and git it while the
gittin's good: though others walk

away with a thousand times as much:

when I was young under the apple
trees, the very whispering of the

breezes seemed the parental (and
societal) authority: so I became

hooked on the nature of things:
when I learned the breeze and the

repression were not the same, I still
did nothing about it, because it

seemed disrespectful to me to criticize
the creators (after all, they (or
he or it) made the apple trees) so

I went right on thinking myself wrong
(in some ways I was) and the superego

right: I've run around supporting,
literally propping up, my victimizers,

establishing them in praise cubicles
when oopsy-daisy they were as screwed

up as I am and made a mess of creation,
namely, me: Lord, here I am old, and

my life of service has drained me,
and I have worked to earn the respect

of those I no longer respect: have mercy
on me: you cannot, I suppose, give

me another chance: right? well, I
never expected it: but I certainly

do wish I had worked through my
adolescence and kissed the past

goodbye (only to return later free
for a different worship:) I don't

suppose you want to hear anything
more about me today: well, you know

after a hard freeze, say at the end
of November or very early December,

ephemerae and moths bound and flutter
about on a warmish day like posthumous

trash: what do these things mean,
starting so late as ghosts when the

hard water is dripping from its
prophecy of what's to come: dust-winged

soft-flown entities, not a bee-buzz
or mosquito-whine among them, the

living dead or doomed, the mockery of
summer, of fall, already shut down,

the crickets stunned silent where
they stood like little cargoes of

Strip

recollection: I don't suppose you
want to hear anymore about bugs:

when I was in the second grade, I
came home one day, and my mother made

me kneel before her aproned knees,
and she ran a fine-tooth comb thru

my hair, and the plump little head
lice dribbled out onto the white

apron: I was looking right at them:
their fine legs wiggled their

relocation about: my itchy scalp
felt so good: my mother scraped away

for days to get the nits: we were
clean people: I caught them boogers

from somebody, but I never did get
the itch, even though a few poor

people came in smelling awful (to
school, I mean) because their parent

had greased them for the itch: one
time a student told the teacher her

mother said "she warn't greasing
fer the itch till adder Christmas":

it smelt so, I mean: better to scratch
than stink for the holidays, is my

opinion, too: I had a clean pair
of overalls every Monday morning:

that's the way it went

if Homer can nod, I can have
narcolepsy: it seems even with Mr.

Stevens that he was a poet when he
was scarcely himself: he made

being verbs of being: his head buzzed
wuz, wuz, wuz, wuz, although,

nodding, he sometimes slipped an active
verb through: oh, but

sensitivity comes of being's
states of being, these linked equivalences,

were, been, was, is, are, be, you
name it: whoever

could muster a hive of *in the's* and
of the's like Mr. Stevens or who could

warp the obvious into half an hour
of tangled nothingness (that

only needed to *be* unbent) like Mr.
Stevens: but Mr. Stevens's lines!

laid like a railbed, tie after tie,
with no sign of integrated

progression but two stiff pieces of
stretched iron: you should see me do

other poets, beside whom this praise
raves: but the tape is too narrow:

the lines turn in on themselves:
they can't get loose, they break

back, they can't lope into loops!
well, they seem to be doing okay

right now: perhaps, I was wrong:
I've changed my timing now to fit

this: we poets endure, become the
source of such curious effects: we

are paid (infrequently and in small)
for that: but heck: for such fun,

even if so little, what fee: I put
my attention, weighty baggage, in

the locker room and try to lose it:
or like one of those little

luggage motor trains, so cute, it runs over
me: anything to get it out or away:

I put it down here on this strip:
I dabble the surface and dither the

image: who is in there: not certain:
but then at least when I strike a

clean mirror, however fearful, I
shout—I'm whole, it's me: I'm

split, halved, but included: if I
get it outward, though, engagement

releases my paint into the splatter-
ing of reality, so many hues and

daubs, such singular intricacy of
who am I and who are you: and look

at us together (possibly), angels
and worms following that: I feel

that my attention, torn down
and thrown out, has been picked up by the

trash truck: maybe it's enfeebled
enough now that it will gentle along

like a drought brook, a small irrigation,
not a tearing up by the roots or

drowning: not a jaguar slink-quick
as shadows in a jungle storm: but

strong enough to beg mercy, peel
apples, and slowly stroke whatever

will love me: none but a dullard
fails to praise the dullard: maybe

not the intellectual dullard as much
as the emotional dullard: the lethargic,

the slow, unexcitable, understated,
the puncturer of loft, the grounded:

no event rising up before him raises
him: he entertains the latest craze

with slumbers: how enviable: one
whose attention cannot quite unravel

itself from dream or sleep or mere
wandering, who cannot focus on focus

whose spine chills with reptilian
patience: go to the sluggard,

thou sluggard, and slug it out

9

the hills are alive with indifference,
a trembling, high-voltage

who-gives-a-hoot: I am so glad I
feel it so strong: they are not

after me, the hills, nor is anyone:
and I am not responsible to raise

them high or treed or consoled:
mountains could bother them: but I

don't care: mountains don't bother
them, though, because mountains,

too, are indifferent, only bigger:
no imperatives are delivered from

the peaks—except, of course, it's
hard to get up them and not much

easier to get down: but I don't
have to follow lofty urgings

ignoring which could bring pain:
except, perhaps—"don't stand below

high boulders on a deforested slope
in pouring rain": I mean, one does

have to mind the constitutions and
configurations of things: pay no

mind and you may have none to pay:
hills, if not totally indifferent

(and, of course, they are) communicate
by abrupt concretions, not words:

I would rather be communicated with
with words, especially since hills

don't have any, and their concretions
are roughish

don't go on about it: put your mind
on love, and let havoc strew its

detritus where it will: it will:
but let that go: fix your beam to

love, which everything befalls and
so little outlasts: learning much

you open up realms to know, but who
knows little knows little to know:

I had to weewee but in the bathroom
I said, is there no weewee in the

weewee-er, but it was because first
thing in the morning a colonic, *but, but,*

bolus of wind gathered through the
night was shutting off the tube (or

tubes) so I just had to concentrate
like hell but one drop led to another

till a tinkle made plenty of room
for the bolus and then everything

eased: later, during a fast walk
the bolus stirred free, too, and

then, of course, I felt fine: how
are things doing: they are going to

change: how will things get: on
the whole, worse, or in the hole,

better: past the worst, things
cannot be bettered: when life is

sweetest it's scariest because it
could go by—it seems to go so

fast—or end: but a great benefit
of misery is that while one might

endure it, one need not cherish
keeping it: funny balances pop up:

one thing certain is the overall
effect: all balances end in perfect

zeros: well, with the exception that
some zeros are bigger than others:

when one black hole moves in upon
another (or they mutually collide)

it has been discovered by supercomputers
working in tandem that the hole gets

bigger (twice as big?): I think a
second grader could have told them

that 1 plus 1 is (or are) 2: I've
known 3-year-olds to do it: babes

in the woods:

the man four-legged with arm braces
isn't there anymore, and the lady
too fat to wobble her knees past

each other, where was she, and Mrs.
Fox, a decisive sharp lady with a
constant near-smile and a fine-lady

accent, where will her like be found
again, here by the waters of the
Inlet, the boats' reflections too

glassy to bob, the gulls crying
downward swoops, the ducks flicking,
drawing those huge wedges of

ripples behind them: but here is a
young man and woman holding hands,
looking at the vegetables as from

another planet, she with a bottom
broad & warm for planting, his
schlong adequate to bed the

deepest seed, and the black dog
licks the baby's face, the stroller
bumping to the plank cracks:

even where the air is empty it is
filled with space and sunlight,
the jabber of buyers and sellers:

those who miss the missing will soon
be missing: Mrs. Fox, are you gone,
or do you wait somewhere in a nursing

home and someone else is preparing
your potatoes, mashing them maybe
when they are already cold: are

you healing, may you return, will we
see you again: we hardly knew you,
still now we realize we loved you,

your face set with a smile, your
quick movements, your choice salad
leaves: the market will leave the

shoreline, the giant poplar will
give up more than its leaves, the
ladybugs all frigging this morning

on the green plant or weed will have
to shop this strange place for
the needed damp: the wind almost

totally missing will show up somewhere
else and sing a different song or
maybe the one known here heretofore

do things close up or close down:
flowers merely close? markets close

one way or the other but not both ways,
maybe neither: knitting knits *up*

"the raveled sleeve of care" and life
closes up or down depending among

other things on your attitude: so
much for my attitude: the trouble

with optimism is you have to be
optimistic before you can be more so:

I've heard that the greatest novelists
in all languages were not good writers:

is that what guarantees Stevens's
greatness: freshpersons confused by

so heavenly a daze would be dismissed
from my classroom: but great persons

need not apply the rules of rubes:
neans (neanderthals)—those ruddy,

brutish, flamboyant little breezers:
nice to have a nest of them in the

basement for quick service but not if
first thing you know they're in yr

wife's suite: stocky, they're tough
to kill: but tout de suite,

cro-magnon with an elephant tusk cd
do away with them, outreaching: I

wish we had them here: I would chain
them up in the basement when I didn't

need them so they couldn't get to
my sweetie-pie: I guess the women

were a little hairier: I wouldn't
mind some light chest hair about

the bases of their boobs: what
afterdinner treats to call the ladies

up the stairs to put out the cigars:
you can't have everything; why not

just concentrate on what you want:
should you miss a trick or trick a

miss: direction imbalances: doesn't
it make hills rise up behind you,

pressing you up into the open, to
think that the fathers amounted (!)

to not quite so much? are you
forgiving of the fathers that they

Glare

didn't create just evil (as you
might have)—whereas some of you

are impatient that all wasn't
created good! alas, dealing with

the fathers is a strong suit:
company chit chat keeps chitchat

cheap

the spirit is universal and without
identity: its habitations, singular

and unreproducible, become slush:
slush and spirit make

the worlds: they have a flare for
invention: they make one of each,

even when they make millions of each:
it is therefore impossible for one

thing to become another, identity
on the one hand one and on the other

unique: if you have arrived with the
pattern and motion to be in the world

then you must leave it: there will
be no need for your like again: I

overheard my neighbor, speaking to
his gardener-helper, say that he

overheard his father say to someone,
possibly a gardener—"The axe creates

more beauty than the spade": I didn't
hear my neighbor comment on this, but

I supposed it meant—pruning beats
planting: the spade, though, is also

associated with plantings of another
kind which, doing away with old

depleted things, may be another kind
of pruning (improving the beauty of

the world by another kind of deletion):
well, anything inquired into gets

mixed up: surface shifts sift out
beautiful language best: it is the

motion not the mark tells: (if I
tried to explain that you wouldn't

find it so easy:) Socrates destroyed
worlds looking for definition: he

found none: by the time such narrowing
locates a carcass, the carcass has

no stomach for meaning: by the time
anything gets that narrow, little

is in it: what is beauty:
you don't know, don't ask: I could

say it is when your pecker rises:
ask your fucking pecker what it

thinks: and beat it bad till it
spits at you: if it spits, though,

Strip

it may be more evidence of the
same thing: nothing having been

explained in 2500 years, we best look
to some other mode of explanation: counting

on the wrist is a classic: smelling
bad turns you away: touching someone

creates belief: the solid world eats
and shifts, I mean, shits, runs in

and out of waves, plays pinochle,
and never says a word: words, their

world lost, the wind sweeps up after:
no dust left, the wind

dies: a disappeared language never
was, never can be, exists nowhere:

I struggle on in this pointless war:
I can't get the rhythms across the

page: I'm narrowed, cramped, sliced
up, pinched between the shoulder blades,

the words spilling off the edge: a
strip war has to be the least

significant of man's endeavors, or
even woman's: but only insignificance

will carry the right significance:
anything worth doing is not worth

doing: I'm just going to fight it
out with these lines, especially

since it's not much of a fight and
the margins are clearly the winners:

Sam Elliott, a destitute widower with
pretensions to learning, lived in a

shack on our farm for a time with his
children—Amaretha, Hessie, Dessie,

Tressie, Lessie Lee, Essie Neater,
Corbett (Corbett's peter?), Metha

May, and Letha: we had nothing: they
had less: one day, Lessie Lee sat

down in the cabbage patch and ate a
whole head because there was nothing

else: raw: I felt pitiful as she
peeled off the squidgy leaves and crunched

them in: they used to boil the
coffee grounds until they were

rust: I remember one day we
were laying logs by the tobacco

bed so as to spread canvas across
the young plants, when Mr. Elliott

said we would have to "undermine"
the log! can you imagine such a

word: we had never heard anything
so sweet and distinguished: also,

one day he said to his lazy (starved)
children, you can rest when you're

dead: well, I suppose so: meanwhile
he had such a bad cold, he would lean

over and squeeze a fountain of clear
water out of his nose: they say

you're supposed to ignore these
aggravations, but I declare I've

never known anything more interesting:
then one day Sam and I were coming

back from somewhere in the mule and
wagon (I was sitting in the back with

my feet hanging out) when Sam asked
me if I knew if Corbett had ever had

any: well, I just muttered: Mr. Sam
seemed pleased at the prospect, tho:

he was on to nature's cycles: I was
way too small: young, I mean: Sam

Elliott is dead and gone: I guess
not much is missing in some quarters

money, enhancing the fluency of negotiation,
has no substance of its own: it

is just medium, action, the flow by
which substances are exchanged,

the system by which desire seeks the
most nearly total and "spiritual"

negotiation between wish and wished-for:
money transmits, transforms, "stands

for," catalyzes—and yet is nothing
in itself, an airy agreement between

desirers, valueless when no longer
valued, iconic and flat when no longer

current: language operates the same
way: it holds its consistences,

designations, forms, economies in
currencies, in motions: let fall

from negotiation, language disappears
as languages have often done, without

any lasting effect to the material
world—the language had added

nothing to and taken nothing from the
economy whose exchanges it had

sustained: write a poem about boulders
or feathers and the net weight of the

world is unchanged: riffle a manuscript
of poems into the sea—one, let's

say, containing much wisdom of human
experience—and the manuscript is

lost, the ink slides free, returning
as much weight to the world as it had

taken from it:

I don't think things go round and
round and come out zero (o), do

you: unless that o is a planet:
seems like there's been no material

advantage to the swirl so far: we
pick up sky detritus, and sometimes

it isn't detritus, if you get my
drift: take that mile-wide hole in

Arizona, and take the blurp when by
the addition of something large, we

lost the moon: let's not get excited:
I do think, though, we've hit on the

reason for a lot of stuff: on the
planet, if anything moves it moves

something else, often backwards:
that scrambles directions so when you

go out to do good, you may get your
boots crusty with evil: and whereas

if you see a guy steal a loaf of
bread, you may later see his babies

chewing (a remarkable mix): that wd
be nice: or if you meet a nice guy

it may be defensive innocence hides
from him his furies: if he's innocent

all the way through, he may be boring
as hell or clear as water: have you

ever tried to isolate the cause of,
say, yeast risings or which seed or

nut riles your diverticulum: I've
wondered what I'm guilty of and

whether an ingredient of my own
brought about the pileup: or there

was the time I recommended to Aunt
Laura that she take a hike, and she

never came back, walking: it's all
because of the mixture, a blur: an

elixir exists somewhere, everybody
knows it: but get it out and where

from: a pure thing, an identifiable
agent, a surefire, not recipe,

element: well, thank the Lord for
the miasma: when we get around to

damning ourselves or somebody else,
let us fumble, feint, squirm, and

Strip

fume: if it's clear, let us be
uncertain why: let us be barely able

to budge off 49–51: sometimes
there doesn't seem to be enough life

left to bother with: that thought
should immediately be displaced by a

better one: life is life, if precious,
precious throughout: add another

pig to the trough, another one goes
off the end: go straight, you bump

into duplicity and deceit: divorce
(bad) turned into divorce (good):

the straight is crooked and the
crooked, straight: go, boy

where do poems come from: you may
want to know: have you ever wondered:

do you care about the baby, not the
fetus: if you're like many people

you don't care about the poem, so why
care where it comes from, when you

mostly do care about babies and still
would just as soon skip the phylogeny:

wonder which comes first, the motion
of feeling, or the event, perception,

connection: oceanward, you could
say that a rift of motion starts in

the doldrums, forms a progression,
but you can't derive what it derived

from: what unsettled a bit of air:
was it air's own weight, a change of

temperature and buoyancy, or did a
wing slice through, or a meteor, or

surely not a neutrino, so tiny: so
what causes anything to start: when

is the beginning of anything, all
beginnings begun: well, that's it:

there's a currency of feeling and it
flows as unformed, if noticeable, as

a drive, and describes a form of
itself, or else its energy picks up

some body here or there and marries
itself to that, creating narrative:

motion, going from here to there,
describes a swerve or arc or salience

and that is form: that is the seed
of form, born in the very bosom of

its substance, which is motion: next
to that, tell me what you think of

a sonnet or some fucking cookie-cutter:
I mustn't become high-handed: I'm

more miserable than most anybody I
know, so don't take after me: I'm

okay when I'm typing like this, tho:
I'm in motion and the worm I am

extruding has a long wiggle: it
seems to me as I look about that I

know some things well: but they are
about nothing: there is no seedcorn,

there are no potato eyes in my stuff:
my poems come out of a little tug of

rift in an oceanic doldrum: it's a
tiny little ship, an airship: fog

could drown it, saturate its jib:
who could get to Mars with that: if

I'm not to have a life, at least let
me tell you about it, that is, that

I'm not having it: that will make
me nearly think I'm having it: imagine

a life! of *words*: better than
nothing, better, better, bitter-bile

better: for what I meant was love:
now, don't blubber: poor comfort,

such poor comfort: twaddle:

I need to get a picture of what's
going on: I'm not—only so far:

no one is: but something is, and I
need a picture of it: a trace, a

spoor, an indication even that might
lead up to an eventual outline, or

in the grossest possibility, something
3-dimensional: a snapshot, really,

before the actual flesh: garbage is
a socialized form: ground up in a

sophisticated, electrical machine,
it flows down the municipal pipes

to the county waste disposal plant
and then out, here, into the waters

of the mighty Cayuga Lake: or else,
paper-sacked, it is set out by the

street in clever plastic, lid-lockable
big containers, and a big truck—

driver and two footmen—passes by at
an approximately agreed-upon time

each week, and the big compressor
blade packs the garbage in: but

litter, litter is without centrality:
it is not budgeted, it flies in the

face of organization, it can be, and
is, dropped anywhere, item unrelated

to item, caught up into the wind or
down into ditch trenches: the central

image of this poem is that it has no
mound gathering stuff up but strews

itself across a random plain randomly:
I don't suppose the universe was

thrown away that way (do you suppose
it was) and perhaps even litter is

governed by certain dynamics of flow
so that it is not truly free: a

heavy frost would keep paper down:
a hot day would dry water off

cellophane: a fall of leaves could
lay some banana peelings to rest:

distribution has its own meeting
places: with litter perhaps the

central image is harder to find, made
of subtler tendencies, harder to see,

Strip

a greater invention than a mere
locale: anarchic and anti-agglutinate,

litter draws one into the resources
of depth, matrix, and vector: one

must learn new forms of containment
or else rehearse the resistances of

freedom

how big is a drop of water: how much
does it weigh: how big is a drop

from a regular, domestic sewing needle
or from a pin or from the point

of a pencil: from the tip of the
finger, a cigar: how does surface

tension enter the picture, say, to
insist on a bead: is there a constant

one could employ mathematically: it
is as hard to be precise as certain:

make room for some big swings in
language: the precious substance is

slipperier than a transgressor in a
mud wrestle: it smears, slurs,

tends, splits: but define a drop
strictly, a standard, reality sloshed

around it in every disintegrating
grade: so that multiplicity and

mixture dissolve categories or else
with really tight, hard categories

the category slips out of material
existence and becomes an abstract

Strip

constant, there where it can be
uneroded by change and difference:

a fantasy I was entertaining this
morning—and it is a fantasy—was

of a naked street, say one deserted
at night or plunged into the early

heat of a new August day (or even the
emptiness one can sense of a filled

street, the commotion continuous,
evened out into a blur): a young

man comes out into the empty street
but nothing is there to engage him:

the sabertooth is missing, there is
no mud-stuck elephant slashing his

trunk about at the verminlike little
humans casting their stings and stones

at the tough hide for a kill: there
is no startling sight of a leopard

overhead waking to the movement below:
is the young man endowed with skills

and violences to find no focus all
day except that of idling around the

steps of his apartment house: joking,
smoking, waiting to see if another

day can end: won't he have to find
substitutes for the life he was made

for: won't violence inside have to
find or make some outside: or must

drugs smooth unexpressed energies
down: well, there are no sabertooths

anymore but what is a man to do when
there are none

it's so cold this morning: there's
a downy clicking bark: there's

starfrost on the windshield: let me
see, now: I've read that one should

never apologize: I wonder if I
should apologize: or should I just

let the evident be evident, since I
probably can't condition that by

begging for mercy: who cares about
the excuses of a beggar—well, I

don't know, maybe I would care: you
know, I take all these pills, every

morning: it's because I've been
sick some: well, I think I lost a few

brain cells in one or two of those
episodes, and one of the drugs makes

me wonder if I'm doing medical
emotions or synergetic emotions: I

think my vocabulary doesn't access
the way it used to, and I don't have

always ready ways to the heights: the
summit of my aspiration has worn

down into a talus of incidentals:
okay? I mean please excuse me: will you

permit me to go on, however I can,
nevertheless: will you add to and

not take away from: I've believed
in you, though I've lied, too, at

times: I've never lied essentially
because it is after all the song that

tells the truth: and it sometimes
lies but its lies are the truth:

the one side of a date seed looks like
an elongated you-know, the rumpled

closure, lips half-met, soooooooooo
inviting: and how sweet the surrounding

meat is! bananas for brains (and a
couple in a papersack) we took off

early for Syracuse: it was 13 and
the trees in the valley where waters

and fogs run were entirely white,
fogs having clustered ice around

every twig: so brilliant in the
southeastern sun: whereas soon

after, as we were returning, all was
gone into a welcome darkness: you

know *all*: *all* is extremely poetic
and perfectly suited to such an

occasion: my vocabulary may be
chary but my diction is still sheer

poetry: I mean, my diction is
poetic: don't you think?

I tell myself to think happy thoughts
but can't think of any: still,

thinking of thinking happy thoughts
helps, sort of putting me on the side

of possibility: not that there aren't
happy thoughts to think if you think

of all the blessings here patent and
available to thinking: misery comes

up with an image or two that blots
out frail peripheries of joy: wait,

wait: give it a little time, stuff
eases by: wait and see: think

happy thoughts: sharply conceive:
engaged as we are with sex these

sexless days—everybody afraid of
everybody else—I have engaged the

pronunciation of harassment as my
special interest, and I prefer

    HAIR-is-mint to
    her-Ass-ment

the latter too precise, it almost
advertises what it condemns: I'll

tell you, language, like nature, will
sometimes just undo itself: what a

narrow strip this walled road is:
shave a micron or two and you're

off-roading: try to get a whole
stretch out, and you get cut back:

see what it will do and before you
can your speed is broken: I declare

I don't know what to do with this
thing, these cramps, this breaking

back: oh, yes, typing is not easy
these days, especially for those

already accustomed to computers:
they can't go back—what? and erase

things or do whole pages over or
type the whole poem over to station

it differently on the page: they
won't do: their backs are sped: of

course, sometimes they push the wrong
button and the hard stuff dissolves

or vandals tear off with a
computer in a hard drive to fly: I

have nothing to say I can't take all
day at, because fifty years of yapping,

what have I finalized, not that one
can't be diffident about finalization:

computers cannot give me back what
I want, which is what neither I nor

the computer ever heard of before:
the happening of something that never

happened, laying it out not so much
that nature can be abrogated as that

its becoming is unencompassed: I'm
sorry, I don't care about information:

I can make up all I need:

if you miss life and get old, there's
no way to unmiss it: you can't,

you can't: pull a switcheroo and
you're an innocent out on a new

stretch: your feelers are as limp
as roothairs, unattached as boughs:

stick with the old sticks—sapless:
play out the rag ends and trifles—

spend the squeezings of the spent:
my wife and I are not mall rats: we

are mall giraffes: we are way above
having any fun, throwing any money

away on junk: we think the people
are basically impossible with long

credit card balances: my wife doesn't
want anything because she already

has everything: however well-off,
she is impoverished of desire: the

other people are, frankly, flappy
with eagernesses: I say, "want not,

want not:" my wife agrees: we
passed a Santa whose ho-ho-ho was so

insincere we considered the power of
artificiality—the deliberately

and emotionally conserving stylized:
so many kids to do a warm globe

around: I'm surprised some of these
men know what they're doing: our

Anniversary (46th) imminent, we went
over to the counter, and I read my

wife several gushy cards, and she
read me some and, aglow with sappiness,

we drifted out, all tucked in in a
bubble: our cheapest Anniversary:

well, we have realized that the
treasures are deep-lying spirituals:

they lie so deep we rarely touch
them but, boy, are they sumptuous!

Janowitz had muffins with us at the
Collegetown Bagelry: she said she

wished those Balkaners would
take a stab at peace!

lawsey-dawsey, it's the sixth
anniversary of my first death, and

I still identify the sweet with
reality, though oft haunted off to

the bulbous rounds and resonances of
the inner world cast out: but no,

really, I'm too scientific to think
"what is there" is really there:

really: I mean, I really hope I am:
I went down the road for a walk

already and found, as usual, some of
the reality not too sweet: a halo

of blueflies over the recent kill,
crows standing about like pallbearers

too stuffed with lunch to
pay attention: and the brook, the

wide brook, chipped by so many pools
and increments, was gone: no water:

not a trickle, just some lessened
holdings, and those holdings

silent: a sparrow
dipped his bill in one cup and

disturbed the whole sky: well, but
you know if one gets down into the

fine, there's too damn much of everything:
but that's how dry it is: how dry

is it, you say: well, it's so dry
that whole trees are dying on the

campus, just dropping brown
leaves and browning out the rest:

but, oh, how sweet to think of
my students: they are young and

trying (and trying) and they are
nervous and not certain, but they

are doing PRETTY WELL: they may be
gone before I am gone, but I will

dream about them out among the walk-
ways, seeking shade or giving up all

the snow: they will flutter about
almost real like scarves

the wind's wearing or like birds
pitching together for migration:

actually, the spirit which was never
anything goes: the rest stays here

I am so ill-stanchioned myself, you
know, just me, that I can't get on

without, like, going to work, getting
away from myself into the affairs

of others, the elevator slowing and
catching still on the remnants of

old floors, plunging easing up: I'm
always hungry for compliments, anything

to bolster me lofty: I consume compliments
like bricks tossed into a black hole

for bottom, a solid floor,
but it all oozes away, *undermined*

by an oily, massive slip: I
should go in the brick business: I

might help myself out a little: I
should throw chunks of old foundation

in there, the steel rods ciliating
concrete: a few bales of ginned

cotton, absorbencies: a couple of
barrels of sticky-wicky: some jungle

temples: a ridge off the top of the
Rockies: that little peninsula that

reaches out from—oh, well: sub-
continent? where there is no love

nothing will take root: the hollow
will not fill: earth's walkabout

will not arise: steps leading up
will not surprise: dreams will

not fog off the higher elevations of
ascension: what is left, after love,

to live with? anger, guilt, anxiety:
I speak not just of the loves of

thighs but of the love of another
more, say, than of oneself: there

are those whom to lose soaks direction
out of the tree boughs, prevents

snow from settling in the granite
crevices, makes daylight an odd

visitor: the stanchions give in,
wither like sea oats in a hurricane:

and then all the world cannot fill
the hole which becomes a trillion

miles of nothing

it scares me to think that being
just me won't be enough to do it:

(I've had a problem feeling like it
up to now) but it scares me

more to think I have to be more than
I am because like I said I'm already

running a deficit: and it scares me
even more to think I could get by

with less than just me: because if
I've amounted to nothing up to now

wouldn't I amount to less being
less: well, but then you have to

think, how well does this thing that
has to be done have to be done:

maybe nobody can do it as well as I
think it should be done: if it's

okay to do it well enough to get
by, why then maybe I'm your man after

all because I'm OVERSIZE Average,
and even the low range of my average

should do to do it: there you are:
the thing is to do it, go ahead and

do it: and see what happens: people
may appreciate it more than you

think: often people expect so little:
there are so many things they're

used to finding they can't do any
better than anyone else: and if

you're really good, they can be
resentful and jealous (and you, by

the way, can be removed from regular
average into an object of some awe

and fear, and people will fear you
then but they won't like you): if

you do poorly but show
resolve and courage, you may attract

a lot of mutual understanding and
sympathy and from a few possibly a

few offers of help: what we have
here, in other words, is some pretty

down to earth stuff in which a lot
of shining on your part may not be

all that appropriate: when #1 looks
up, there is no one to look up to, and

Strip

when he looks down, he has no equal
and no friend: he attracts,

quite contrariwise, sleazers, weaslers,
pleasers and outrageously impertinent

nobodies who think they should be #1 and
have not once imagined the bad

side of that, be average (or a little less)
the wide world of the average is the

widest world to inherit, whereas
splendor lives by itself in a place

of icy mirrors and chilling rooms

fracture the mirror and don't ask me
what becomes of the world: the world

too is fractured but is still
unfractured and the mirror, now,

has no truth to see except its own,
its own splits and deflections: it

loses touch with possible mystery
thinking (thinking?) it has found

some in obfuscation: it's a mystery
tho that obfuscation can show how the

world really is beyond its simplicity:
I reject the North because it is not

my native ground, and I reject the
South because it rejected me, and I

reject European clutterment because
we fought to put that ocean between

us: I identify with no sort or kind:
I am by myself: with me is the

thinking up and writing of this poem:
I am for the poem: it tells me who

Strip

I am: as the poem becomes itself,
so, I hope, do I: it is sad and

simple, yet true: if anyone loved
me, or if I loved, I would be loving,

I would not be writing: I have not
found anyway yet to be what I want

to be: I'm looking: I'm writing as
hard as I can: did you ever hear

anything so pretentious: I tell you
the defensive can come on as stilted

and askew as a peering, preying mantis: shows have
put me up so high my hardest thing

(!) is to get down where I am, and
there are leagues below where I am

to relish: but it's not my feelings
but how I can change them, is it?,

to bring about the same changes in
you: not that you don't have your

own feelings: but you are, as I am
like a moray eel, sticking out only

a little: however fine the eatery,
the scullery's behind a door:

heads or tails: ups or
downs: tops or bottoms: heads and

tails: ups and downs: tops and
bottoms:

Thank Goodness

how wonderful to be able to write:
it's something you can't do, like

playing the piano, without thinking:
it's not important thinking, but the

strip has to wind, the right keys
have to be hit, you have to look to

see if you're spelling the words
right: maybe it's not the thinking

but the concentration, which means
the attention is directed outside

and focused away from the self, away
from obsessive self-monitorings:

these self-monitorings create problems
where there are none: they fill

inanition with misery, when if you
can look about and do things,

inanition goes away and so does the
misery: but I, I have a long history

of misery: I've suffered enough, I
should know how: it has come off and

on often enough, I should expect it:
but sometimes it has gone away for

years and then the return is difficult:
I have to (you, one has to) learn all

over again how to cope: one thing
one learns, I suppose, is that there

is little poetic value in writing
about misery: so many other things

to most people are more interesting:
almost anything is: a few of those

little rug moths fly up this time of
year and light on the walls: I get

some of them with a fly swatter, but
I don't know that that helps cure the

moth problem: when do they mate:
when do they lay eggs: how do they

know what to do: they probably do
it without thinking: the way I

write: I write to write: it's
not that I think that's the way to

write: it's that this way of writing
occupies me: it's a way of existing

that is more comfortable than not
writing: most writers, of course,

take pains, as I'm sure they should,
to write and to write well: I don't

mean to say this is good in spite of
my nonchalance, and I don't mean to

demean the reader (what?) by asking
him to spend his time on time merely

spent: since I started this, 15
fairly pleasant minutes have passed:

my gratitude for that is, like,
boundless: I am encouraged to think

that maybe I can get through the
whole weekend by writing when I need

to: when I can't find anything
(better?) to do: believe me, I wd

not do this if I were better connected,
if I were better engaged: walking

is good, but the knee joint in my
deveined leg hurts (the whole leg

swells in the heat): swimming is
nice, but I gave up my membership

when I got sick: reading is sometimes
possible: when I can read nothing

else, sometimes I can read what I
have written (that's usually innocent

and nonviolent enough): I've said
before that I write so I'll have

something to read, and that does
double the pleasure and the time the

pleasure takes: I am basically in
perfect health: but right now I

have things in the future to do that
seem like a threat: these things

are not threats but exciting
opportunities: I have just twisted

them around to where I'm *afraid* I
can't do them, and that is threatening:

as a matter of record, usually when
I do such things (such as poetry

readings or dinners with presidents
(of colleges or universities) I do

Strip

them well enough to make people
kind: what could be less threatening

than kindness: it is much less
threatening, say, than love, which

is so invasive and deeply involving:

two of the birch trees have got
their tops loose from the snow and

have risen into the air like monsters
awakening with feelers: they lean

and reach for higher air: if a front
comes and the wind jacks them up,

lifting and catching them up, then
they may be restored to a new

tranquility of poise: this is the
rising of the burden-bent, you know;

the realm of the playful, overseeing
heights: let our heavy emotions

become such tickles way up: is it
the same, being guilty and sinning;

then we are sinners: we trust that
in understanding and forgiving,

or really trying to forgive, the sins
of others, we may understand and

come as close as possible to forgiving
our own: but as with all verdicts

there's something more to it:
verdicts are fences in fields where

lava flows

I know most people like to stay
alert: there are a lot of little

hopes and treats they want to be
awake for: for me, I regard

drowsiness as a state approaching
grace: the druggist says, don't

take these two drugs at the same
time: they might cause drowsiness:

how much drowsiness, I say: do you
mean you pass out, or feel a little

sleepy: and she says, no, you would
feel sleepier than with one

alone: that tickles me because I
never felt drowsy enough from the

one: it is so wonderful for me,
often, to have the troublesome

world ease away: I yawn a
little, nestle into a corner wall

or big chair, and snooze:
half an hour is great: an hour

exactly twice as good, and all day
practically incalculable: but

judge not me as you must not others:
some of the drowsy-looking people

you see have had so much food, sex,
and sleep that the only sign of life

on them is a tiny smile of dumb bliss:
you can hardly get through to them

with a question, such as, could you
get somebody to turn off that loud

fan: sorry, they say, question mark:
they don't even know the custodian

is shaking out the dust mop right
over the cookies: some of them, of

course, are on drugs, not the ones
at the pharmacist's: but ones you

can sometimes pick out among the
lilies of the field: everything is

beautiful, they say, in its own way:
I don't think so: victimizers are

not beautiful: when they do things,
well, one's spine grinds with gritty

ice: but in the arc of arising or
in the depth of reaching down, it is

still true: each of us, even you,
even I, considered in the full

shadings of our dynamics, well, we
may be like what the Chinese

philosopher said about water, that
it never makes an esthetic mistake:

but I think the water of this movement
has run aground: I don't know which,

if any, part of the foregoing I
really believe: like water meeting

an obstacle, I will have to go around
or under it, or rise above it:

toodle-oo

oh, we go to Owego some Sundays for
brunch at the Travelodge by the river

and pass Brink Road, (on the left going
over (and on the right coming back)):

oh, we plan to go today—it's early
now—and the snow's leaking at the

eaves, so the roads won't be frozen
(except in higher elevations): I

love the weather, its moods and elements
are so much like life: often, if I

don't feel just like the weather, I
feel the opposite: sometimes when

it's mild, I get cranky, and I had a
student once, Wendy Zomparelli from

San Diego, and she said she couldn't
stand it when the sun came out *every*

morning:

my hands that in their motions used to
out-steady boulders dribble now

the coffee at my lips, especially if
I've trimmed a bush or talked too

long at the market with someone, one
of those plastic bags lumped weighty

from my arm: but enough about me:
what do you suggest: I mean, have

you ever experienced such a thing,
or do you ever expect to: it's not

too bad, actually, I mean it's suitable
in time to tremble with, at, or over

something: it can mean that you've
survived long enough to know surviving's

sticker-shock: you always expected to
have to pay, however willing to

wait: go on credit: interest-free
and if your payments fall beyond the

pale, why, who's paler then, creditor
or thee: I bought myself something

once: three ceramic elephants in a
row, the biggest ahead, the smallest

behind (!): they cost eight dollars:
I like them because they are mine and

because I had to pay for them: but you
can have them, if you like: I'm in

two ages at once, the giving way and
giving away: but no more poor

pitifulizing me: I have plenty and
give plenty away, why, because here

at nearly 70 stuff has bunched up
with who knows how much space to

spread out into: but no more bogging
you down in my tears: no more

talk about my tears: tears and
fears, I mean, and hopes and dreams,

and the dream of loving and the
dream of being free, free and in

love with beauty: but let's not talk
about me anymore: what about your

tears: and fears: what do you
waken at night into the middle of:

turn her over and saw off
another piece: I mean of the log

she is snoring lean: help out: be
useful: prize enterprise: enter:

Einstein made things as simple as
possible and no simpler: let him

have the simple: I'm pure: let's
not talk about me: how are you doin'

I'm glad I don't have fifty years
to see these limbs hung with this

snow: I feel for the bushes,
burdened; I feel for the birch trees

bowed: the heavy, dripping clusters
grow more with new snow than they

melt: it is ridiculous: nature
having poured it on pours it on: so

patient, so still, a test to the
limit: wait, wait for the slow

procedures, the long unloosening of
the branch tips from the ground:

maybe so that nothing tears, not that
snow won't trample to tearing, not

that ice won't hold the tips till the
tree tears away to rise, the little

twigs sticking up torn from the snow:
as I say, I say, whatever you say:

also as with a quill (or stylus) I
plink upon my machine outmoded as

hell (I hope hell's outmoded) and
meanwhile a quiver of the flank in

Strip

Sumatra quivers a flank in Jersey
City, cellular love quickening half

a globe (you can't get a globe away
from anyone, isn't that fortunate)

away: love finds a way: European
clutter, those relics of decayed

aristocracies: here in the sweet
lap of a brawn-bred democracy, we

have fresh aristocracies of our own:
what will be their relics are now

expressive: altruism is somewhat
placid, it meets and engages into

ease: warm, soothing ministrations:
but the negative emotions—envy,

greed, aggression—are sharp drives:
devise an economy to engage and

express these, and the economy
bristles, the high polish of desire

used up in making: an economy is
the means by which the undesirable

is transformed into the desirable:
the nobel prize for nobility is

surely mine: I simply will not let
things go bad: I push tragedy aside

or try to to clear the way for a
touch more hope: I mount the hope

on the high, jeweled sway of elephants
and ride through the streets casting

gold coins about: people, I cry, O
people, I say, try to get over it;

check dawn out; put in a fall garden;
boil the water; keep your peter

clean; listen, it's not over yet—
the fat lady had a bad cold, another

is besent for: things will change:
you may even learn to live with what

has already happened: that will be
a new start: oh, yes, if I rouse

the rabble they will cry me up till
I win a sizable nobility that will

sustain me in luxury as long as I live:
let's be realistic

I feel it is so necessary to get
ahead of somebody and so unkind to

do so (and humiliating not to):
maybe that's why I feel more *ex*

than *dis* (tinguished, I mean): I
can't go right straight down the road:

a wheel comes off and runs across a
pond: the hood flaps away to Mars:

the seats disjoint into ticketed
areas by a theater: pretty soon, I'm

riding a chassis like a Greek chariot
plunging downhill to a bifurcation:

no, I have a lot of trouble with
singleness of purpose or precision

of direction: I want to roll up the
whole landscape like a piece of

oilcloth and take it with me: this
means I encounter fullness: well,

more than an armful or chariot tare:
(I should use an unusual word

occasionally—unusual is a funny
looking word, though (ain't it):

I see the eye-level silver shine of
the axe blade the big neighbor carried

at our house at dawn, and I see the
child carried off in arms to the woods,

see the sapling split and the child
passed through and the tree bound

back: as the tree knits, the young
rupture heals: so, great mother of

the muses, let me forget the sharp
edge of the lit blade and childish

unknowing, the trees seeming from
our motion loose in motion, the deep

mysteries playing through the ritual:
let me forget that and so much: let

me who knows so little know less:
alas, though: feeling that is so

fleeting is carved in stone across
the gut: I can't float or heave it

out: it has become a foundation:
whatever is now passes like early

snow on a warm boulder: but the
boulder over and over is revealed,

Strip

its grainy size and weight a glare:
rememberers of loveliness, ruddy

glees, how you cling to memory, while
haunted others sweat and wring out

the nights and haste about stricken
through the days: tell me about it:

the truth laid bare is a woman laid
bare: nowhere does the language

provide the truth humped bare, as
with a man: the language travels

close to the bone: sometimes when
you're up against it a few bucks will

get you all the way in: already
top-heavy with bloom, the chrysanthemum

in the yard pot has sprawled broadside
with snow: I hope the pot didn't

crack: that's a nice pot: the
flat-out truth: why am I always

afflicted with things you can't find
like "the poetry section": "pets"

is plain enough, and "young readers"
and "occult": tucked away in a

subdivision of a nook is the poetry
section: sure, *you* find it: but

the salesgirl in the 30%-off section
revealed a slight swell lateral to

the cleavage, but in the 75%-off
section, shaving (or plucking) was

notable along the delta edge: I was
never so pleased in my life: I

bought everything (though I was
actually looking for a book on rhyme

—no such luck): but I love women
so much, even the way you can talk

them into duplicity, I mean their
melting spirituality, like the

rose-warmth of nursing, just moves
me so much, I feel like saying,

please excuse me, but are you sure
it would be all right if I mounted

you: that harsh and greedy move,
with wholesome respect not sufficiently

acknowledged, and the entire enterprise
not sufficiently floated in tenderness?

Strip

I don't know about you, but I think
tenderness can be observed even in

the eagerest strokes, so that when
it gets rough it's just as free and

easy as playing with the wind: I
bought a pair of shoes for ice: a

gritty or cusp-crested sole suctions
the slick: the man behind me, a

young fellow with his wife, had an
extra $2 coupon he gave me: can

you imagine: I wished him and her a
Happy Thanksgiving, I was that

thankful: this strip is so narrow:
a rhythm cannot unwind across it:

it cracks my shoulder blades with
pressing confinement: the next time

I take up prosody, I'm not going to
take up this

the poet's wandering finds another
way, but just the thread of another

way, not a path, road, or superhighway;
not an airstrip or launching pad—

and that's why the so-called
Emersonian self is not "imperial"—

the solitary self is alone *in the
world* with a consciousness directed

toward all but by only one, one little
guy seeing and saying, not speaking

through the megaphones of public
structures but if to anyone to another

alone, one to one: if those ones
add up to millions, still they are

single threads unbraided

she said, it's hard to have hope
when there is no hope: she'd run

back and forth looking after people
till her legs wouldn't work: she

would send her legs a message and they
either wouldn't get it or wouldn't

do it: she just lay there, poor
thing: I told her to have hope: she

said there wasn't any, or not enough
to pay much attention to: she died:

the adopted son she staked her life
on was shot dead by somebody at the

7-11: just a month or so later:
she didn't know about that: I reckon

she got off just in time: you'd be
surprised, though, how folks can get

over something like that and keep
on trucking, if they have legs: she

didn't: nope: but she didn't know
anything about the son: pretty

lucky: old lady

one types to please and appease, to
belay the furies, to charm the real

and unreal threats into a kind of
growling submission: typing is this

ancient skill, now so rare it is as
if priestcraft, intoned knowledge in

the legend of words: this idle skill
is an offering, symbolic in kind,

a tribute to the makers of fear:
oh, we say, look at this typing:

note the actual ink, the pressure of
the keys against paper: isn't that

we say, curious: don't you find it
distracting: doesn't it recall to

you old rich worlds you'll be all
day recovering: meanwhile, we

typists will be eased enough to have
dinner, maybe take a nap: paranoia

is just a motive for operations, for
recognizing this and that and thinking

how this can deal with that: it is
a sharp acquisition of knowledge:

it gets you up to the plate: with
all the strikeouts, you may learn

to hit the ball: no telling what
you'll be paid for that, and it was

all sort of magically accidental: you
were trying to do one thing when you

did another they pay you for: is it
not better to be comfortable and

ignorant: then Love and Trust, arm
in arm, waltz by and assure us that

there is nothing to fear, that, indeed,
the people like to look at our typing

just because they like to: they have
so much friendly feeling they delight

even in the fearful mirages your
typing rigs up: think of that:

it was all the time all a show: it
gave energy to the occasions: it was

something to consider: but, of course,
you know, some loves are despised and

some trust is deceptive: separating
out the threads of reality, you may

become entangled and fearful: you
may have to override caution in order

to believe in love, to make a, as
they say, commitment: appearances

dress reality in different
guises: so, you are asking, what is

my advice: my advice is, it's not
going to be easy, or else it is going

to be so easy you won't even know
it's happening: take a chance, stay

alert, have faith: how do you do
this: I have no idea: you "work it

out?" you remain compliant, yielding,
assertive, angry, grateful, cautious,

and type a lot: you can't type
without dealing with the roller, the

return carriage, the space bar, the
margins, the ribbon, the paper, the

keys—not to mention thoughts and
feelings: so it requires some attention:

the great thing about attention is
that you basically have only one and

Strip

when it is occupied it is hard to
preoccupy it, and that is why they

say the merciful Lord gives us only
one thing to deal with at a time;

that's because we can pay attention
to only one thing at a time: you

may hurt in a dozen places, but when
your mind settles on one place, the

other places retreat, distally vague,
unvisited: choose the positive

where it can be found or invented:
for no reason but that it feels

better than choosing the negative:
but choosing is not easy: you have

to work at it little by little: one
little bit enables another, so the

effect builds up and you wake up one
morning calm, at peace, or happy:

at least, one hopes so: do the best
you can, do

logs, limbs, and branches lying by,
tugged off the street: the side of

the street looks like the aftermath
of a logging: but today, oh, today,

the temperature has gone to 37 (that's
Fahrenheit, son) and drip-drops are

falling everywhere, the birch slips
arching upward out of their burdens,

readying to snap their tresses loose
from the ground: you know, that

dense ramification of twigs birch
go off into: goodness, if you could

just throw poetry away the way ice
crystals fall out of the trees:

imagine if there could be so many
shiny centers in the, yep, setting

sun (actually, it's still about an
hour up): oh, if only the brook

could not make any sound unless it
were filed away in the museum: the

wind when it blows, and lately it
hasn't, shouldn't be allowed to

Strip

trifle with so many leaves: and I
mean leaves, because believes it or

not, *leaves are still on the trees!*
snow came before frost this year,

hard frost I mean: so over by the
hill next to the bridge, snow bent

leaves over the road as for an arcade:
the traffic had to one-line

and slow as through a tunnel: it was
most remarkable, like reading a poem

by Stevens, somewhat brittle, and
truly trees were cracking and splitting

with loud report and hissy-splits:
there is just so much to learn: so

much: one thing you could count
is the birds: they've flown: up and

left: no song: and the crows play
with air currents but silently like

monks swimming in the pond, or monkeys
in the hot springs: this is the

fourth day

the petunias are, this morning,
bewept with dew: they focus intensely

downward, their pale undersides topside,
overarching flops: still, but, yet,

indeed, it's rained, in a summer of
the least rainfall ever, the lawns

ghastly dry, some leaves falling before
fall, the lilacs crinkled yellow,

the ivy ever sere: fungus and mold,
I suppose, have been put to rout:

that's probably good long term for
roots and general soil condition:

but the ground cover (pachysandra)
looks wilted: so when

I got up this morning and saw
reflecting pools of rain out along

the road's edge, I did a passamezzo:
there's a breadperson down at the

market I could look at all day: you
may think I have said breadperson

Strip

because I shouldn't say breadman or
because I wouldn't want my wife to

know if it's a breadwoman: I can't
say one way or the other because

that would be gender differentiation
and might suggest that looks have

something to do with taste: but I
can't stand and look at him or her

all day because that would look
foolish and he or she would start to

notice, and nothing is really quite
easy in the world: I can't even say

what I would stand and look at all
day: we are tied round with ties:

and lies: we are lie-tied and
tie-laid: the world is ashen with

flash and burn, desiring and desisting,
reveling and retching: why do people

not want things eased away instead of
wired to the highly charged: is the

disorganization of the languid so
scary: not, for me, as scary as the

crises of fear: tranquilized—oh,
that has been my missing paradise

so long, and its lack too long my
hell: with nothing, thank goodness,

to be miserable over, I'm miserable
over nothing: but it makes no difference

what becomes of me now because I'm already
become of: unless, of course, I could

write a good line: I could spell out
my dream along a good line some beauty

might take a turn to, and then we
would be toe to toe on the floor,

the music swaying us and educating
our wishes and edging us toward the

closure that is our temporary but
essential solution: strip typing is

like strip mining: you peel the
surface off things shoving clutterment

Strip

downhill, heaping hunks, spewing
grit, filling cracks, riddling shale,

making news out of old geology:
massive millings: my strip typing

says little but can be understood:
whereas, many things so dense they're

very meaningful are hard to know:

I guess it's *because of* the downward
slide of everything towards entropy,

the momentum of the downglide, that
forms are like foam cast up onto

floats of pause: if this is not
true, I do not give a damn: I must

die: that is what unsettles me:
the reasonable/unreasonable dynamic

of that, the popping up of bubbles
that pop: makes sense in the local

but why may I not dwell somewhere in
luxury besides heaven: material

tries to make it to eternity but
recycles, and spirit that forever

was forever is: forever, possibly,
because it isn't anything; that is,

it's nothing, or else it's something
time doesn't fool with: equilibrium

will not do what disequilibrium will
do, the slope, the values of the old

mill stream: then there's the mill
pond to swim in, dark, diamond water,

so still, so deep, such summers! I
can tell you right now: I can figure

it out but still resist the figuration:
I feel like I would prefer not to

comply: but silly me, that's because
I've forgotten how grateful one can

be for the permanent ease that does
not know itself: what a comfort,

that from here, there is a way out!
and as a boon addition, no way back:

it's right, I suppose: I suppose it's
right: right or wrong, we string

along: talk is cheap: it's the only
thing I could buy enough of to fill

up this tape: and talk is action,
and the mouth is an image, booboo:

the trees are still bent, downloaded
deep: white weight: more trees

have splintered and resplintered,
branches closing roads, whole trees

lying down, root-reared: naturally,
nature adds dearth to dearth, pure

calm holding the frail limbs sprung
as a bow under the evil wet: in

nature, nature brings rescue to the
rescue after every damn case has been

given up: then, slowly say, the
snow compacts to a risen degree and

a drop of water drops from the clump
and then another drop drops: sometimes the

trees are like people, they just
don't have that much time: but it's

beautiful, and tonight ice will come
back where water was: some people

move to Florida: others wouldn't
think of it, think of it

the strong want to live on the edge
but they are so strong they can

seldom find an edge anywhere: while,
alas, the weak inhabit edges everywhere

and seek strength anywhere to pull
back away into safety: how sad

that what we have is not what we want
and what we want we can't find: if

you say what you have to say then you
have nothing to say: therefore the

unsaid is the lens of observation &
what will not tell itself will not

be done with telling: stripping is
what I do, keeling to this band of

paper, a fleet rig on a round-the-world
and back-around-again: it is so

arrogant to say it is not important:
imagine the gall, asking to be known

for nothing, or to be known for having
the gall to ask to be known for nothing:

what I want is not something out of
something—fairly easy—but something

out of nothing: a difficult, primal
figure: in what was space made: if

space closes up, what is left behind:
if this universe bloomed through some

integument from another universe,
where did that universe come from:

presence only annihilates these
troublesome questions: springs and

kangaroo rats and insect bites and
reed mats and dinosaur teeth: lots

of stuff, begun and ended over and
over, so that the loam of our lives

is a loam that was life, flesh from
flesh strangely begotten: flesh into

flesh, a soilure and a soil: but the
wonder of such infinite devising—

tadpole and caterpillar, mushrooms
and figs, mole rats and chimpanzees:

five million insects and only a few
white rhinoceros: ladybugs and plums:

the list lists it is so weighty:
just mud and information: enough

oohing and aahing: everything taking
and being taken—provender: the

lacewing fly, something's meal: the great
quantity of things lies elsewhere

can you make nothing interesting:
what is the first thing you would

encounter on the first rim of nothing:
why, a smell: a kind of a smell:

that's right: I reckon: smegma
afloat in the round of a bauble of

pussy piss: that is vulgar: that
is so vulgar: Wallace Stevens wd

never say anything like that: or
think it: or smell it: I do not see

how the technique of poetry could be
reduced farther than this: so this

must be the rim bounding nothing:
smegma, though, is probably populous

under the microscope, the dead paste
of epithelial cells would be a living

broil of carefully crafted life:
there must be something closer to

nothing than smegma—or even the
smell of smegma: think how complex

smell is: a single whole piece of
smegma, one part in a million parts,

capable of alerting nerve ends in,
you know, the nose: there you go:

dragging in a prominent structure
already, a face fixture—oops, there

goes a face on a head on a body, no
we were going the other way: I tell

you, you better be ready to look
about before you find nothing, it

may not be so easy to find: people
always talking nothing, wonder

if they've ever seen any: we have
weather enough this morning without

a forecast: (snow midNov) the upper
branches of the great trees weightily

woggle: the birch bunch tips over
to the ground: the shrubbery skews

and splits: no birds sing: all is
closed: nothing is left uncanceled:

getting about is as much a hazard as
a hap: I'm trying to think of nothing

(the forecast is for four to eight
more inches) but even nothing has a

rim around it, which makes it a
something: still, somewhere within

that something is a "float" of
nothing, a kind of resilient blob

wandering strange: pure nothing: the
nothing right next to the rim might

be something but not farther in toward
the central nothing: if you cut out

a specimen of that, you would have
a piece of nothing, but then the

"piece" would have to be entirely
mythical or it would be something

again: it's hard to care about these
arduous ardors when the eggs are

nearly over, and the snowplow is due,
due and late: and branches

crisscross the street, bringing down
lines (O ye, in the future, can you

imagine, our landscapes (along our
streets and across our fields) are

strung with wires, phone, electric,
high-tension, so primitive!)

Strip

nature's disasters trim nature up
shipshape (it *is* a ship): high wind

which we had last week cut dead wood
out of the trees, though it's so

early in the season, the lilacs still
hold their leaves—so much worsening

the burdens—and today's snow brings
down whole diseased or overextended

limbs, so the trees get skinny and
light, their catchments shrunk like

sculptural wire: ocean-bottom
storms of lava make pretty islands:

cracking faults make room for oceans:
continent drifts into continent and

crinkles up razor-young peaks:
nervous mornings produce so much

speech: pacing helps, too: I am not
patient: actually, twigginess has

not been helpful for some of the
trees: really twiggy trees catch

heaps (and heaps) of snow and bend
way down till their branches crack

off or they pitch head first: on
the way to the campus a while ago,

I came upon a log across the road &
on the way back, a tree fell across

the road right in front of me, and
later on Highland a bushy branch hit

me right in the windshield: I said
to myself, if I don't get on home!

everything now is in a still, white
suffering, an unloaded tension, I

mean, a tension in which the load
has not been un: and the tension

makes me tense: I don't like to be
cooped up: I don't have any *Snowbound*

resources: my typewriter's my only
outlet into this cramped-up strip:

I don't get any easing away before a
margin cracks me stilted or forces me

back in on myself: when I use up
this tape, I'm not buying another:

this is a dot upon which what
has happened has happened

sometimes I get the feeling I've never
lived here at all, and 31 years seem

no more than nothing: I have to stop
and think, oh, yeah, there was the

kid, so much anguish over his allergy,
and there was the year we moved to

another house, and oh, yes, I remember
the lilies we planted near that

siberian elm, and there was the year
they made me a professor, and the

year, right in the middle of a long
poem, when I got blood poisoning from

an ingrown toenail not operated on
right: but a wave slices through,

canceling everything, and the space
with nothing to fill it shrinks and

time collapses, so that nothing happened,
and I didn't exist, and existence

itself seems like a wayward temporizing,
an illusion nonexistence sometimes

stumbles into: keep your mind open,
something might crawl in: which

Glare

reminds me of my greatest saying:
old poets never die, they just scrawl

away: and then I think of my friends
who may have longed for me, and I say

oh, I'll be here the next time
around: alas, the next time will

not come next: so what am I to say
to friends who know I'm not here and

won't be back: I'm sorry I missed
you guys: but even with the little

I know I loved you a lot, a lot more
than I said: our mountains here are

so old they're hills: they've been
around around 300 million years but

indifference in all that time broke
itself only to wear them out: my

indifference is just like theirs: it
wipes itself clear: surely, I will have

another chance: surely, nothing is
let go till trouble free: when

Strip

I come back I'm going to be there
every time: and then the wave that

comes to blank me out will be set
edgy and jiggling with my recalcitrance

and my consciousness will take on weight

every now and then I drop a bead of
rolled snot in the philodendron and

mold grabs it in the eagerest flare:
first thing you know it looks like

a hairy dead daddy longlegs: last month
I planted a piece of peeled apple in

there and several days went by before
a growth intensely green at the soil

level took it over: but then the
apple, weeks later, got too dried out to

nourish its vanishing, and the peak
part still stands shrunken but white and whole:

I should dry up: stripping
down is like being worked over with

mold but, dry, one finds where form
finds everlasting: because usually

you know, spirit is temporalless:
throwing in a few new words & stuff:

should have said *timeless*: but
everybody pronounces that: another

Strip

choice is to give one's sweet water
to the undoing and not mock oneself

finally with permanences: the great
sharp-pointed aspiring stones one

sees in graveyards along the road,
well, one understands the grief and

loss and the great wishes, but, below,
the face has drifted into a twist

and the bones have soured sticky:
the unrollable foundations above

topped with a spire or flight of
angels are such a laugh: such a

big laugh: but then what a nice note
that is, life a big guffaw,

possibly, even, a celebrant guffaw,
possibly a word to us all: I hadn't

meant to get off onto a happy
note, but life is just irrepressible

even in death: it all comes up
again and starts over: why give

Glare

a millennial hoot: the hills around
here are three hundred million years,

repeat, old: rather than see chimpanzees
in terms of ourselves, I would rather

see ourselves in terms of chimpanzees:
rather: what a funny looking word

rather is: tah

will I will the will to go on—what?—
from here, where does going go, except

to gone? oh, I dream in this wise,
now, yes, yes, yes—images—the

body bent to the cane: some way I
may get away: below neutrality, the

ease of neutrality looks good, a
positive: we've had some rain,

dribbles at midnight, the rain pipes
thunking clocks: but the ground

is wet only two or three inches down:
below, summer's drought persists:

not that many of these slate-slabbed
hills have more than 2 or 3 inches

of ground to wet: roots crickle the
stone granular: but no soil, loam:

when rains wash, they wash the grit
away: naked roots touch into pools

of unsoaking water mineral-enriched:
first frost is possible tonight:

we're peeling the last of the peaches:
the trees are smirched dry-red, frost

Glare

or no: tomatoes, you know, the vines
wilt right down, cold-bruised stems:

the seasons roll straight ahead,
swaggering from side to side, cold

to hot to cold to hot: time that
takes away every second it gives

goes straight, too: we are not in
keeping with its round bubbles or

animal balloons: though we see
ourselves too short to bend, look

how our figure 8 contains infinity:
our figure 8 Möbius keeps two sides

on a single side: don't mess with
us: we know we're doomed whichever

doom it is, here or there: our
cousins the gorillas, a sweet people,

I wonder what they know: their eyes
seem blurred like the eyes of our

anxious: have they peered through
too many leaves or eaten too many:

familial troops with big daddies:
too much submission to the shoulders

Strip

of the red stick? I'm sorry, I'm
sorry: I do not feel that obfuscation

is a good cover for mystery: no,
mystery is what comes true at the

center of the perfectly clear: I
mean, all efforts at clarity having

failed, one succumbs to mystery:
but merely to screw something up, or

scribble over it, or substitute
something for it—that is perverse,

mere perversity: mere perversity
resulting in the unintelligible is

not mystery but a neat trick one is
not likely to get away with for long

the yellow leaves left on the
birch flip in the wind like

butterflies trying to pitch: when the
wind lulls they light, then dance

like frit in the sun when the
wind's shiversome again: if you're

fortunate enough to live as long as I've
lived, you may be as old as I am: awake

some mornings, I don't know whether
to discharge a gun or an obligation

battalions of leaves routed by the
wind scurry to defeat: smegma flakes

off the chilled penis: a chipmunk
pauses to dampen a stone his own:

a robin or so left stands erect at
dusk, too stuffed with honeysuckle

berries and crickets to budge: so
the big surprise is, fall has come

and all the banal transitions are
running their changes: and what new

has one learned—why, that the leaves
that served have been dismissed, if

not torn, from the branches and by
this we learn that in falling we are

puzzled about what we took or gave:
did we just play the DNA through, if

we did: was there a high form we
shamelessly enhanced: was there a

current otherwise unannounced but
for a peppering of people: or did

nothing give a shit and we fell out
here the way a rock could appear in

the sky: whatever: taken a day at
a time, I can tell you the way the

sun first tipped the treetops gold
this morning, and the way we found,

some of us, our dicks on waking hard,
and we so hungry and all—what a

great opportunity for roaring
exultation: but then, the ball can

whip a right angle out of the cup,
and where are you, where are you:

or nemesis riding a 60-year-old
memory can sweep through wiping the

the bark off your bushes: how did
I, for example, mistake this place

as a place for ease, when the place
itself shifts, boils, drowns, shakes

worse than a teenager: I guess if
you were to compare the two best

poets in the country, it would be
like comparing apples and bananas

missed by every movement, exile of
every glare-ridden trend, never the

tissue of any issue, I traipse to the
bookstore to see if I've arrived in

any index, not, notice, as a relevant
subject, but as a slur, since one's

hunger gets even down to that: no,
no: in Nature Writing, nothing:

nothing in poetics: unbeat: well,
I've proved Emerson unimaginably

wrong: one *can* live in one's time,
and lucky for it, with no involvement

in its politics: I love the chicanery,
fraudulence, expedience, greed of

the political (read, human) world—
those allow, those qualities, for so

much invention, unprescribed variety
but my time line, such as it is,

shears the peaks off politicos'
peaks: I'm not in Nature Writing

because I've been too deep in nature
to notice: nobody noticed: oh, well,

it was enough to see: except on a
cold, windy, clear Sunday afternoon

with not a damn thing doing: then
one's heart longs to be noticeably

dismissed, at least: in the still
pond of nothingness, rock the boat

or there won't be any waves: someday
I'm going to write on how Stevens

makes his *be* buzz: I am: scram:

if I don't know what it is it could
be anything—a slue-footed, coned,

tail-bent galligarngion: so it is
helpful when words pinpoint, trimming

excess: this tape is so skinny: I
have to crack off the lines and roll

the trimmings back into the next line:
there is never enough room: the

lines have to digest something, pack
it down, shove stuff together: my

wife has a trimmings doctrine: she
thinks trimmings should be removed

from the premises: raked-up lawn
grass, leaves, dead branches, old

rose canes, squirrels' walnut nibblings:
she doesn't believe it's right for

a red oak to have its leaves: she
doesn't think anything should find a

way back into the ground: she doesn't
want to wait for no "slow burning

of decay"—as Mr. Frost would say:
rake it up, she says, get the blanket

under it, pile it up by the road, let
them haul it off: mercy, I think,

what the hell's wrong with letting
a little natural stuff help hold the

hill together: or why not see if a
little loam can drift out of decay

into soil and regrowth: but, no, it
won't do: rake it up, clean it out:

strike the *v* out of archive and you
have another archie: well, we just

finished driving to Chicago and back
and we's tired: oh, yes, yes, yes,

we's really tired: plumb tuckered:

life has left me beaten up and beat
down, yet, I confess, I am neither

beat, beaten, nor Beat: sorry to
disappoint you: I have every hope

still to turn into a decent, moral
creature: the sky's broken but cold

this morning with a touch of rays
splintering through here and there,

little threads or gauzes of threads,
mixing with hanging currents of flurry,

bridal veils for the marriage of heaven
and earth: a glorious, cold, early

winter morning, another beginning,
sweeter (and cooler) than the first

morning of mornings: who knows how
primal succeeding days can become:

some (many) through time have expressed
an interest in world dominion,

minions from software manufacturers
through all the stages of hardware,

bullets and shafts, even saintly
philosophers softened into gods: I

Glare

declare if I don't think that may be
a good idea: what appeal from a

short, meaningless, jailed life should
one announce—a willingness to go

along and take it all or an arousing
desire to cast limitation aside,

greeting the unaccomplishable
unaccomplishingly, a work never done,

a surrender intimated only at the
setting out: hark: why buy in to

the world's soothing controls: why
yield and smother: why the lying

silence: why not say, this is what
I want and never be without work in

not getting there: but puling
compliance, how sickening, sucking

up to safety, behaving into honor!
ass kissers' noses are in a crack,

their eyes abutting butts blindly:
whereas the bright face addresses

hills from the clear summit air of
mountains: ah, but the lowly, the

lowly, they seldom kill, they are
unthreatening, they are shining examples of

having less than we: are they not
innocently adorable: I am not beat:

to be beaten is not losing while it
loses beating

this summer the weeds, even, and
trees dried up and died: the mullein

on the back slope stalked out with
shriveled leaves and the little

flowers keeled over, the only way to
go: oh, this tight strip breaks my

rhythms, loosens my stable tables,
pours everything toward the middle

where it runs off, a streak: there
isn't room enough to lay something

down flat: speaking of flat, the
only thing that recommends Ohio is

that Indiana follows it, and the
only trouble with Indiana is that

Ohio is left over: out west from
here around Angelica, Cuba, Olean,

Salamanca, Bolivar, and Jamestown,
the reservoirs of the Alleganies and

the pools scooped out along built-up
roads have so retreated into themselves

that hardly a snitch of water remains
a heron can wet his toe in, and

Strip

the big empty bottoms have sprung up
a fur of grass: looks like a lawn:

the fish and things are nervous as
hell: the congestion, I mean, is

worse than traffic into Chicago, the
big limousine-type trucks thumping,

the double-exhausts over the cabs
chuffing black, the smell of roasted

coffee (just burnt gas) all
over perdition: what is there as

much fun as a trip:

breaking up the hang up hanging
awful in the mind, that is the procedure:

finding the form of the process, the
mode, how you go about dissolving

the knot (that burns your feelings)
a sort of lightered knot tar draws

out of, a knot that spits and pops:
fire's a solvent: faster at times

than water or psychological breadth:
the form forms and if you're empty

space only, the form is open
to artificial, say, irrational, say,

mad fixations that drop into your
bowl: arrange a full life or

the terror of emptiness will fill
emptiness with terror: love's the

best filler but isn't cheap and
anyway money can buy only a semblance:

if your forms aren't full of love it
doesn't matter what they're full of:

Strip

I do the best I can and god, I suspect,
does the same: his plans allow for

the emergence of the unexpected and
attempt amends for the consequences:

I am in this way made in his image:

so here I am fist-diddling in the
poot-shanty when my grandmother

appears at the door—surprise!
surprise! she frowned (this is my

grandmother poem) and my sex education
was off to the races: well, there

were other problems, too: for example,
I found through exercise of my 11- or

12-year-old sexual rights that my
glans penis wasn't free of the skin

which kept tearing a little from time
to time and getting sore: sex was

in those days a secret, something
that never happened: I lived with my

sore penis right through sunday school
with no one to tell about it to:

but it came loose all by itself and
through use gave me in time one nice

looking thing, if I must say so myself:
really nice: I mean, perfect: not

quite as big as wished but nevertheless
a considerable consideration: I

wouldn't take anything for it and
wouldn't have then, either, grandma

or not: it worked out fine: this
is probably the beginning of my

confessional phase: you see, I am
just as lowdown good for nothing as

you are, maybe lower: I'm so lowdown
you'll feel great thinking you've

edged me out: go ahead: one
thing you don't get in the movies,

porn flicks, girlies is the smell:
yep: smell-free sex: in fact, you

get no sex at all, just head fucking:
I do not complain: you'd be surprised

how little something can be and be
better than nothing: and there are

notions sometimes as persuasive as
the flesh (and less smelly): but it

is degrading to think of sex as the
flesh because in true love it is the

spirit that connects, and the feelings
are divine, tending toward the sacred

and they generate children, sweet
little innocents in a sense:

in this life if you scramble into a high
place you have to fall out (of a high

place) but from a low place
you don't have far to fall: in either

case you hit the ground, but in one
case it takes longer and

you hit harder: the difference,
already noted, noticeable:

    old molly hare
    whacha doin there

    runnin thoo the cotton patch
    hard as you can tear

    old molly hare
    whacha doin there

    runnin thoo the cotton patch
    fartin like a bear

I don't know who holds the copyright
on that: my father used to sing it:

a peanut is a pea, not a nut: and
the difference between a watermelon

and a sweet pee is, you
recall, twenty minutes: other

names for peanuts are groundpeas and
penders: also, if you slip into a

low place, you haven't had far to
climb: arch up: an undistinguished placing

conforms more nearly to the reality
principle: the distinction that

lifts you above the fortunate
attracts bullets and clay-makers

and money whose fluidity dissolves
centers: lie (lay) low: frugality puts

you above others (and comfortably
below your resources) but interests

few: hardly anyone resents or desires
frugality

if I say I did it, did I do it or
did someone else do or say he did it

or did I imagine I did it or that
someone else did: or did someone

say he heard someone else say he did
it: I take the pieces of action where

I find them: judge them by the
curvatures of their unfoldings, by

the reasonableness of their scripture:
it matters importantly who something

happens to, I know you know, and
if something was done, it can mean

a lot if you or I did it: so don't
get me wrong: sometimes I did what

I say I did—if memory serves,
memory filtered through by invention

and displacement: responsibility
bears where it can be placed: so,

oh, yes, I stick with a sort of
reality: but let the writer go:

let reality come true if it can at
the center of his fictions: let his

dreams be as if histories: let what
went before come after: but I didn't

do it, I didn't do it, they cry,
sometimes until they gurgle in the

rope or splatter the blade—and
sometimes, what's more, they didn't

do it: mostly, they did: some that
did it laugh all the way home: it's

hard to distribute justice fairly:
injustice happens: money talks

one good thing about being too late
is like too late to worry: it's too

late for me to worry about making real
money or getting to be well known or being

loved: another good thing is by the
time it's too late to worry, one has

accumulated enough pickings, shreds,
passing fancies, busted hopes to lie

down in, enjoying the drowsy
disengagement of incompletions,

blocked adjacencies, and discontinu-
ities: what the hell: what was

there ever to have won anyhow: an
hour of sun: a leaf gliding toward

a brook: a pussy hair behind your
ear: can't you just imagine what

sunlight does to the high polish of
a high executive suite, a slice of

late light cutting across the carpet:
it's almost better to have somebody

Glare

to have nothing with than have
nobody to have something with: the

value of things slides: Bill
Gates probably can sit among

windows and feel shades, nothing
in the world his money can't cheapen:

whereas the hungry child seeing the
dipper spill into his bowl knows

the world's dark deliciousness: you
can die starved from too much as from

too little but let's vote
precautionarily for too much

fall is here: crows are up in the air,
like leaves: they arouse

clusters of argument, squalling out
quick turns and dipping fluttery as

if shot: the wind loosens crows and leaves,
I mean, and nuts hit the

ground and water jiggles in the brooks again:
do you care for those tightly woven,

Strip

gutter-rutted, stone-thick, unutterable
poems artifice sets up

to stall the mind: well,
I often do: overdone, it gets funny

though: a shuttle scuttle

stars, too, are often twinkle-eyed
with tears and their after-midnight

lights shine through windows, lights
lasting till dawn's rising voltage

puts them out: brothers try to
commit—or do—suicide, or sisters

waste away with eating disorders:
wouldn't it be nice if the troubles

of the world spared someone: then
we'd have miraculous ones to look on

in happy disbelief: husky ball
players lose their touch or endorsers

pale away: and the general gravel
of the cosmos, no one even notes

what becomes of that: only stars
give point lit high enough for us to

see the widespread evenness of
disaster: of course, of course,

there are thrills and kicks along the
way: and stars illuminate those,

too: we let stars get away with
plenty of roughage because we do

appreciate this focus: in their
lives we see writ large hilarity &

happenstance out of control, as with
us: and so we do submit our wishes,

our longings that rise into
recedings beyond stars to local dust

in a street sweeper: we nestle and
nudge till we get down: we dicker

with our own dicks and G's and sip
the sweet readout of difference

into nothingness: we thank our
lucky stars for their help, but ever

more we thank our unlucky for the
low, low rhythm that holds the world

together, apparently

you dragass around: you know you're
on empty: the light has gone out on

your vowels, blue-lit with hallucination:
the slick has dried on your rhythms:

the pulp of your poetry has drained
juice-clear, prose having

decided what's to become of everything:
it's like, well, if, like, you pull

the wings off a gnat, you have a nit
or nittwit: but, of course, keeping

on is the only thing to keep: stop,
you sink through: imagine you can

knock up a knockout, or knock a
knockout up: redress and re-dress

the backdrop: though it's neutral,
breezes fan, snakes strike: but it's

neutral: project upon it filmed
rights: play or play with your

piano: I have the dominant gene that
curls my tongue: the

trouble is that it then looks
like a sow cunt: I look in the

mirror and think had I a boar's
needledick I'd do it to myself in the

slitified tongue: this enables me
to project recessiveness and "get"

the echo of mixed emotions: (the
major macroeconomic is that more

people sweat a raise than raise a
sweat): easy reversals lead

to wisdom: the great practitioners
on Wall Street take a different

tack, a take tack, no, I mean: for
example, you run to the computer

every day and buy and sell and lose
your money, whereas someone takes

the long view, does nothing, and
gets rich: also lives long because

his belly is not entangled, just full:
takes all kinds: you be the kind

not already taken: be doing something
excusable, like for mankind or the

arts, and under that shield get rich,
be greedy, don't look greedy: this

is really good advice, coming from a
skeptic. who taketh up poetry picketh

up an unemployment form:
poetry's the wealth poverty

buys: some of the wealthy have bought
poetry but were poor in spirit or

their parents sucked and they learned
to: the great thing about brooks is

that water moves like jaguars and
gazelles but is dead: the dead unless

ruffled by worms don't move and dead
impounded water except for a nibbling

fish or two doesn't move: but water
which is like stone, dead, dances and

sprays, flashes and dives like life:
and what is so good is it is immortal,

immortally dead forever so it can
keep on forever going away and coming

Strip

back, a great action at no expense
to life, the sun an engine long-dwelt

in the heavens: but not a dweller:
just the spirit of motion animates

water: it glistens: we are ourselves
pools in a long brook: husked, we

glisten, too, glisten and glisten

we'll just be here while we're here
and then we'll just be gone: things

will appear uninterrupted either way:
while we're here the figure we cut

will be as if vacant, and when we go
the cutout we left will cave in on

itself: alas, but still, still
we cry—do we exactly understand

that this was the way it had to be
(yes, of course) or is this a trick

maggots, too, fall for: what are the
maggots for maggots: dinky little

molds and bacteria: no, nematodes:
some kind of flat worms: something

tiny that squirms: maggots, tho,
mostly—as we do not—turn into

something else, flies, you know, with
wings: that's probably where we got

the idea of angels from: we'll fly
away or flies will fly away with us

or seed us with fly seed that turn
into little blunt-ended nuzzlers:

a meditation like this is somewhat
melancholy: hopes of setting a bit

of stuff aside out of the round are
founded like other hopes on hope: we

pour in the formaldehyde and brick
bodies up tight from rain and stuff

and more stuff but stuff happens and
earthquakes and volcanoes and cutting

floods grab stuff back into the swim
and motion cannot be prevented from

getting back whatever stalled in it
a "moment": our white wings will

catch updrafts and we'll float about
effortlessly as vultures but have

trouble pitching in trees, clumsy
brogans no adaptation for chicken

feet: we'll land flatfooted on rims
of the deepest canyons and we'll

pitch off into the air: we'll sing
and glide touching wingtips and just

keep doing that: I suppose: how
can leftover things keep building

up and not deprive the circulations
of their soup: alas, it is all made

right: I'm terribly sorry: it is
made right

it's a brisk, bright fall day and
from these two campus chycks passing

by, I hear, "I'm always so uncomfortable
in my winter clothes." what do you

make of that: I'm always sort of
snuggled up in mine: it's the winter

outside that feels uncomfortable:
but they're thinking ahead (they're

young; looking ahead to discomfort
isn't as uncomfortable for them as it is for

me, say): but is she more comfortable
in fall clothes: if so, even more so

in summer clothes: how comfortable
would she be in nothing: if there

is nothing in the heights but nothing
I suppose we can dismantle the arcs·

and get down: hello, folks, here
we are down here with the pills and

pressures, shoe polishes and handsaws,
leaking faucets, and TV shows: our

longest view is to the next meal,
sex event, pay day, job: what,

what is certain, not to mention
certain to last: what, is there

yesterday's pie and tomorrow's pie
but no pie today (the man said,

whoever the man was): curiously,
it's down here where there are so

many things that there's so little
to say, whereas the heights, which

hold nothing, conjure inexhaustible
inquiry and dream: plenty to think

about: sidled aside, I shuffled
about for anything that might do:

do you suppose there is Noone in the
sky: has Hubble spotted nothing:

is it really true that a dust cloud
is collapsing somewhere (so slowly)

that will center out a sun, perhaps
with remnant planets, and everything

will start out all over again
somewhere else: and is there nothing

left in the whirling dark star but
whirling, that hard dark body whirling:

Strip

my goodness: are we merely here:
are we only a mockery the light will

never miss: I saw dogs catch a
squirrel on campus today: well fed

they just mauled it and didn't eat
it: later, I passed close to look

upon it and a blowfly, bright metallic,
was pitching about on it: I think

that whatever cares for the squirrel
was in the squirrel and somehow

failed: the fly "cares" but the
dogs are gone, doggone dogs: other

squirrels were not in attendance:
when something dies you might as well

forget about it

see a penny, pick it up, it's 2¢ (and
the IRS spurned), considering taxes,

village, city, county, state, federal,
school, and sales: I cried out to

the heights in my misery, and the
heights said, cool it, and said,

can't you see I'm making and colliding
galaxies and stuff and watching the

watches (I mean, clocks) and over
there a 150,000,000-stretch of

light years is turning to plasma and
something is always going off like

popcorn, a peppery popping of suns,
or a smacking of wobbly stones

long-dwelt in speed: so I said,
listen, okay, I get it, cool it: &

just there in that wrung moment I
understood the guiding principle and

started scaring up a little supper:
hey, you never know: you could win

the lottery or your poems could come
in for something, your bone could

harden, or the sun could do itself
in, a quick quieting: I would say,

go ahead, call out to the heights:
it couldn't hurt: the heights,

unmollifiable, continued, listen,
this cut-up method will not work,

I can't be spoken to this way and
what was it you said anyway: one

could go on with this: in the
beginning, it was easier, I think,

to begin than it is now: there was
some say one big pop, after which

complexity quickly ensued: whereas
if you began today, you would be

faced (figuratively) with an estimated
unenumerated 100 million species:

whereas there were no species at all
at first: when mud separated into

water and rock, then there were three
things: and light: I just feel so

broken down: there isn't a bit of
room on this tape for a little

Glare

expansion or elaboration: sculpture
becomes grit: kidneys, tubules: a

blinding lack of scope and sense's
fracturing frit: but, of course,

when everything runs, nothing runs
through your mind: the total

answering makes no world where you
can see the carriage rounding the

bend: streams need to break in on
themselves into banks and tend, this

way or that, noticeably apart:
everybody knows that's what holds us

here forever limited, forever fragile
and not forever: there's a bump on

my rump, right in the abyss of my
yss

have I put my input in: if not, where
have I put it: I've written so much

I think I must have put in my input:
but every morning afresh, I feel

unexpressed: rain in the luminous
woods, yellow with unfallen fall,

feels like creation beginning: and
gulls foraging on the lawn by the waste

treatment plant blur in and out of
form through windshield

rain: I always supposed the better
place we go to was better because it

was better: but, of course, it's
better because it's no place, nothing

at all, an end to this place:
that's better: now, the furniture

of forever, the terra celestial, the
gold streets lining puffy clouds,

the throne, the streams that flow by
(benches, hammocks, somewhere to lie

or sit down)—oh, well, I don't have
to do away with kitchen materials

Glare

because I never think, and never
thought, of kitchens: a clear

place—O Blivion: I still like it
here: learn to love misery, confusion

and you better here considerably

sixty years ago, I used to hear every
Sunday that Jesus was coming: the

preacher wasn't specific but said it
could be any hour or minute but

certainly before next Sunday: next
Sunday would come but no Jesus, and

the preacher never seemed embarrassed
for his disaster quotient was as high

as ever, and certainly something had
to happen before next Sunday: Jesus

was coming, the good people would be
caught right up where they were,

fishing or frigging, and the graves
were to fly open, the nice people

winging away, and the bad folks about
to get it: well, all this will do

well as a statement of the provisionality
of things, a warning not to rely on

any morrow but to check out today:
I guess that's why the congregation

never seemed alarmed to be there but
skittish about ever being there

again: after all, it's what the Bible
said: and most of all it sounded

right: a sky rock the size of Rhode
Island, already on course if a million

years off, is probably what they,
I mean the preacher, was/were really

worried about because it might hit
any minute: but the boats this morning

down by the steamboat landing, now
the Farmers' Market, bobbed barely

in the boat shed, each boat in its
stall standing in water quiescent as

the giant bulls in the bull barn after
a draining emotional experience: (you

know how they run out the artificial
cow, mounted on something like a

slender wheelbarrow, all of which the
bull mounts, willing, no doubt, to

be fooled but worried something's not
completely right: what, tho, won't

a creature do for a little relief:
no telling how many times the bull

has to come *every* year: but that is
an unworthy verbal effect: the bulls

are royalty, prizewinning ribbons
cascading down their stall doors:)

but it was pouring rain this morning
after months of dry weather, and the

boats appeared sulled in their booths,
adoze like the nearly satisfied

bulls, but the people at the market
were mostly missing, a cold rain,

an anxious rattle of rain on the tin
roof, the greens still not hit by

frost: a sense of an imminence, a
change, snow pellets in the higher

elevations: we need to think of the
power of prevention and the prevention

of power

well, it's true, I'm from North
Carolina where there's precious little

ice skating, but we do get brittle
little crusts of ice on puddles and

stuff, you can crack it, pane thin,
and eat it like a wafer: slips in

your hands and freezes your fingertips
but so cold and good to your teeth:

I know why I write in this method:
if I don't write what I'm thinking

right then, it slips my mind: yep:
gone for good: sometimes, the next

day, or several weeks later, I have
a thought that has an air of

remembrance about it, and I think,
gee, this may not be déjà vu exactly

but I think I've been down this
street before: I remember now that

yesterday morning or this morning
when I was coming back from the

campus store with a mocha chip muffin
I was thinking of the word *cramp* and

Strip

I was thinking how this tape cramps
my style: it breaks down my extended

gestures: it doesn't give your
asshole time to reconfigure after a

dump: everything happens before its
time, interrupted, turned back, cracked

up: but yesterday or today when I
thought of *cramp*, I thought of so

many mots juste to go with it, but
now I'm trying to remember a memory,

the words juste neither to this morning
nor to now: anyhow, I am brittlized,

run like a cow through a cow dip, my
flourishes stripped down, my feathers

deflowered: so cramped, my words
lose letters on the right-hand edge or

I start typing too early on the left-
hand side and slice words up: I

keep thinking, oh, I'll remember what
that word was supposed to be, but

I've already told you about my memory
but I figure when I xerox the strip

onto regular paper, I'll fill out the
words in pencil, so a typist can get

it right: what, though, is right:
wouldn't it be better to let the words

come out of and go into breakage in
the usual way we, too, come and go:

wouldn't it be truer: wouldn't
accidence be bodied forth into

revelation: have you ever heard a
whore moan (hormone?). . . .

when the trees tug trying to hold
the wind back (or, more accurately,

when the wind nearly sweeps the
trees away) do you suppose the

resistance each leaf, twig, branch,
trunk puts up and communicates to the

roots thrusts the earth forward into
faster rotation: or, if not, and

there are just the right number of
winds in the right places, does

contrariety resolve into no effect:
or take for example, since the earth

takes hold of nothingness in the
highest atmospheres, is there no pry

pole (I mean, no station) the pry
pole can get leverage on: even if

not, cdn't it be true that since all
the energy derives from outside the

system (the sun, for the most part)
why couldn't winds persist in certain

areas and directions to make the
earth sail the way ships do, the old

kind of ships or recent racers: just
so, though the scope collapses, my

contradictions blow me about but
perhaps no more than turn me around

spinning me nowhere, no tours, no
plane or Amtrak trips, just a sort

of top digging down, screwing in:
screwed in far enough, I might (wd)

find turning trying and then the winds
of my sentiments would just wear

themselves out and me as if I were a
stob: do I contradict myself, you

say: well, I get interested in both
sides of the argument: I am unhappily

not an either/or person but a
both/and: I have more sides than

two: I have so many they round off
like a glazed stob or bead of water:

enough about me: I sure wish I could
think about something else

Part Two

Scat Scan

well, it's true, clarity is in the extremes,
whereas truth muddles in the middle: of

course, nigh onto everyone wants truth to sidle
over to where clarity is, but on the trip

qualification trips it and exception douses it
and contradiction split-chunks it and clearly

what arrives at clarity as truth is so
yellowed-weak with travail that it is just often

sent back in disgust on a return trip likely to
wear it down to nothing: what are we to do:

whew: desperate to make a dollar, some guys
on the outskirts between farming and

handymanning will borrow into front-end
gear for snowplowing and then one or two snows

fit to plow will hit the whole winter, and the
guys go under: nature is subtler than a pound

of spiders: and the next winter, likely,
bankrupt, they sit buried behind their long

roads, while we, unused, break our backs and
hearts on shovels: our destructive rage

against the unmercifulness of nature has
put us in need of saving environmentalists, who

have perhaps never happened
up on a nest of rattlers: we had to

tear down half the woods to have a door to keep
the wolves away from: don't tell me that

fetches of wind and slugs of rain erode the
fields; where is the cabbage to come from: and

are we or are we not to give a summit or two
to the iron ore of skillets: language plays

upon what-is the way light plays on water: it
is without substance (as light nearly is):

moving, glancing, dipping, cresting is its
veracity: the ghoulish light on the water of

cisterns, tomb-stale: the flitting flickers
of flinty ice crystals nearly too light to

land: the honey weight of heat waves: evil
shakes in the shadows it shuns the light to

find: light apparently travels in the dark
becoming visible as the object it strikes, even

the deep blue heaven on those sucked-dry
skinny-bright days the commingling of light

with atmosphere: (alas, the once great Mozart
is now Muzak): my science may be right or

wrong but telling you about it is the truth:
all this dithery dawdling, I can't get going

you scan the surface and not a crevice
springs light forth and no dark trench

invites you in, so where is the exploratory root to
fix, where do the stakes that angle up the

spread stand off: if you can't get going you
might as well get gone, goodbuddy:

    the snake dangled from the
    woods of his loins and, tempted,
    she offered herself,
    and the snake rose to the sweet
    fruit of that occasion,
    after which millstones of
    labor and kids-to-raise swung
    from their necks, and they
    awoke way outside of paradise. . . .

there are those who think it okay to be the
way they are: this conclusion has never

reached my case, nor has it ever it: not even this
plan, this possibility: I bring you one—

who?—dragging himself behind: up front
moral conflict, chicanery, sleaze, and

shtick ruffle the terrain, while there, in
the rear, oh-oh the unprotected, uniform self,

Scat Scan

clear, dumb, whispers a single
word: counter that with all this talk: how

tiny the seed can be whose pulp is the world:
(I should never criticize anyone because—

so there be no loss—I glue the fault to
myself): there is, there are, there be: there

is the chance that: it is this that: wuz wuz
if I am never to ease into the fame

groove, I must at least secure the virtues of oddity:
should a pip squeak: or should

one wrap the whole world round in a film of
disbelief and swallow it: the crow convention

in the tall trees downslope yesterday (big-berry
boluses) was somewhat unsettled, shifty, and

quarrelsome: sudden callers would pitch into
breezes and round back to a new perch: two

would slice downward in an aggressive pairing
disagreeable wing-flickerers would lift and

relight—250 of them altogether and once or
twice they all lifted off at once

downwind like a loose cloud: and then by
twilight, unnoticed, they'd left the trees

picked clean: what sort of meeting was it:
was the whole genetic neighborhood assembled

to see and be seen: were the early stages of
mate selection under way: will they pair off &

square off, now: it's 10 March: the redbird
has been whistling and chipping since mid-

February: small, bud-feeding birds have
cheeped and sat still, fluffing themselves as

in an adorning mirror: how do the birds know
what to do, what it's for, where to build, how

to care: how does the butterfly, bulged out
of the chrysalis, know what to do, having

been nothing but a worm: it is a mystery:
but no more a mystery than that I have a

planet to sit on while I type this: that
there is a mystery there, son: shore is: if

you take anything seriously, you're a fool,
and a fool if you don't: wherein,

then, is one to be wise: 'tis wise to be
foolish and foolish to be wise: leant over,

scrambling, searching for the last years, one
goes into a pixie dance at the lunatic poetry,

the wooden structure wrapped in butcher paper
meant to save one from death but, alas, it

was but a painted show that careens and crashes:
hark, here goes the squeaky thing again. . . .

hang on—oh, hang on—to our frailty, oh,
don't lose hope: the brain will be improved:

scrawny bits will be fiddled free: where the
bear used to roam inward, fear will otherwise

be focused (or dispersed): the deadly ambush
of the toothless tiger will no longer sanction

alarm: we'll get our hopes together: we'll
make it all up ourselves: we'll outtake the

IRS, confront the diagnosis, assuage the shunned
lover: we'll demark a height we could scramble

into the emptiness of: we'll find some place
to go not round and round: oh, look upon the

look of the bodhisattva waylaying wayfarers
with enlightenment: or if that doesn't work,

we'll invent endurances, anxieties, tests,
losses anew to keep our souls sober and gravid

with metaphysics: hark: we will go one way
or the other or plow out a median: hang on,

or let go: dissolve with ease or resist and
spit: just think: if I'd stayed on the farm

I'd be a happy holy roller: instead of this
smart boy: this shaken isolate, this drained

discard, this dust bit, too disconnected to
settle, this comical comer touching down

here and there on a surface too hot to stick
with: but, unrolled, I still call on the Lord:

I do: I say, like now, Lord, I just discovered
there's something to ask for besides to stay

here: not that I'm asking: and not that
You're (necessarily) there: but if not, why

You're my Top Wishbone, my #1 Wishing Well:
You're my Everything: and my everything is

nowhere near all there is: what shitty talk:
I phoned my sister (there's only one, now)

last night: she lives in NC where clear
skies (which we didn't have here) enabled her

to see the blue-blur comet: she said you could
tell it wasn't a star: blue: said it was

over by the Dipper handle: I don't
like the close-by of these things:

and the unlit ones, the asteroids: I don't
care for them: it's the rocky mindlessness

shining in high speed: the pitching roll:
the possible pelt of the big landing: I don't

like things that "show up": suddenly, I mean:
and we with no units in outer space to

misdirect them: we're like some beaded braid of
aphids and some animal comes along and eats

the leaf: so long, dear ones: and what
becomes of Mozart then, I ask you: and are

mathematics (the several kinds) destroyed: is
mathematics then something that isn't: I love

so many people (and most women even more)—but
I don't say anything: not a word: where, I

would like to know, would that get them: tits
to woo, clits to consider, floral warmth,

what's not to love: desertion, withdrawal,
blame, responsibility, child support: hey:

with women there are fewer things to
play with but more to be in

I confess my confessions never concern the
truth: I confess for dramatic

substance by which I hope, like Shakespeare,
to entertain you from distraction: I am so

pure, so to speak, that I feel at home mostly,
as you may have heard, in the severely empty

heights, way up there, just coasting over
content: you may be sure if any nipples are

lipped or clits nipped, it will be in the same
way Shakespeare shakes Dick III out on the

stage, a wonder: I am not, however, much for
the wine of life, let's say, as is WS: I am

not for blood, let and loved: I confess that
I have not yet seen a robin (24Mar): others

have: I confess that trying to lose weight
disestablishes me psychologically: but I wd

not present you with murders, mummies,
and marriages: that is grown up stuff: I'm

sorry: I must just see if the pond will dry
up: and weep for the squirmers in the oily

leavings: I must not proceed out upon the
stage and chop anybody's head off, though

there are a few people I wouldn't mind jeering
half to death: S. didn't really care, as I

don't either, about any of that "content": he
just wanted to squeeze the syllables and feel

them slide: oh, he wanted to hear the truth,
that is, the accuracy with which the syllables

slit the throat: the way a Hail Mary arcs the
field and lands accurately in the fleet hand:

all this is true, and lies keep it bright

no use planning for the future if you're not
planning on a future, or not much of one:

rib-it, rib-it: the money you lavish plowing
through the death facilities would have looked

good as wine and roses: early wine, though,
is bought with slender money: and as for

roses, choose the wild: well, it's Easter
morning right now, with a nor'easter,

out-of-whack, whipper-jawed, eight-inch dump
load of snow on the ground, and it, as they

say, agoing to snow: surprise, surprise!
hardly anything so far rose compared to what

fell: an illustrious, time-consuming irregularity,
a dingbat of a dumbball, a porous containment,

an outsized scrunch, well, a parfait miracle!
an appropriate misalignment, a straight line,

limp, a wonder to be told: sometimes, perhaps
often, people need only be outside the

normalcy of perception to be original: they
may be as dumb as the next one but they are

noticeably so: painters, for example, who
don't understand that the bottom of the picture

represents the ground don't know where the
people in the picture should seed the corn:

a brilliant piece of consequence (which, as
Johnson says, is not the same thing as

subsequence): more learned than I let on, I'm
less creative than I should be: but I'm at

least as creative as notice so far has noted:
my entire life, stacked up behind me, seems

sad: does yours: I often wonder if other
people recall joy: I recall that there was

joy but the recall is sad: what a small,
spine-skinny, creepy little piece of

ransacked misery I was, day in and day out:
I turned every bright tomorrow into yesterdays'

grief: maybe any day used up is worsened by
no longer residing potential in the future:

the hope of copulation turns into a lack of
hope of copulation: somewhere in between,

tho, a rusty lode swims free, a momentary stay
against profusion: so that's what it's all

about, just *now*, that just went by: oops: a
dip in the dance, a leg underneath, a horse

collar on the sheep: snickering at the funeral,
laughing at the defloration: I know not what

course others may take but I'm for run-over
stationwagons

HELL IS ON WHEELS AGAIN

it is so much easier to become known by doing
bad than doing good: shoot

a president, derail a train (killing several
unexpectant people), bomb a plane or big bldg,

kill, sodomize, dismember, and cannibalize a
string of people and the pressure on notability

will build up: but try to improve peoples'
morals (preachers) or instruct them in knowledge

(teachers) and the news will spread slowly:
of course, consequences vary: for the bad

there is a lifetime of retirement (with
study and physical exercise) guaranteed: the

good sink away into the inadequacies of Social
Security: for there is an hierarchy among

criminals: get a parking ticket and the devil
is to pay: open up with a repeater in a crowd

and you get a private escort and suite: those
who do important things are important: the

rest is left over: the old fat man at the Easter
brunch said to the taller old fat man, my

bowling days are done: probably, his balling
days are done, too: the old have time to mull

things over or maul things over, depending on
the history: but should one enter into the

coral-fan immediacy of the present, into the
skinny filaments of ice with thaws coming:

should one hold back from his time, cowering
in long-range views: the tragic commitment to

now, should it be urged: should I push my way
all the way out to the periphery of definition:

out to where the thinning is mist, the risk
high, the taste keen, the present drawn forward

and backward into itself, now, just *now*, just
now:

THERE ARE PLENTY OF SEATS
UP FRONT

I tell my poor pitiful graduating MFA poets to
cast a hundred résumés out upon the environment

and maybe one bread source will be returned to
them: (fellow says he doesn't mean any harm

probably knows he's doing some): (I'd rather
be a misery than a miss): the man from

Audubon is coming, to profile, defile, or maybe
just file me: I must think what my meditations

will surround: first, we artificialize nature
then we naturalize artifice: oh, when I do

come on close to my nearest native thoughts,
my dearest figures and feelings, I can't bear

the trampling out through keys into trolloped
letterings what others might snicker with or

at and I, with my floundering ineptitude, might
only precisely debase: hark, indeed: I sidle

off into the peripheries where speech may be
bluffs, and echoes may have mixed with woods

and brooks their recollections: I can't tell
you what I care about: I care too much: can

you listen around the edges a little, if you
care, and take up anything you find and want

Scat Scan

as yours : because I feed in the periphery to
secrete the kernel, I have an abundance to

give without end, because, because it opens to
the world and drifts back away to it: so you

can know nothing, I tell you everything:
but everything may surround islands firm enough

to land on or lights strong enough to make a
course by: it doesn't matter if you end or

begin with me but that you have a journey of
your own: I'll be the mirage the camel's legs

flicker in: or I'll be the caw of the crow
broken loose at night by wind and thunder:

I'll be around: I'll be the bark you flatten
your hand against as you lean a look into the

grand Grand Canyon: be on your way (with me,
with me) and I'll have my way alone to myself

with you: when my journey is done and I am
gone on the other journey, earth's, not mine,

you will look back at my hollow meanderings and
then know everything: after all, a

trail of nothingness marks its way by cave and
cliff, drop and steep, shore willow and fern:

no, I carry hods, I'm a sideloader, cement mixer:
I deal in avoirdupois, millstones swing my perfect

neck (low), I lumbersomely sway: I carry
weight: but the tug of the encircling

sings me to the storm drain: am I about to
be or am I being moved by the waters: will

the speed climb as the circles shrink: has most
of my world gone on before me: is this it:

is the voice of gravity calling up through
the grill or grid or whatever it is: should

I be turning around to cry goodbyes before
I'm too busy whirling: alas, another,

perhaps the original, hole "black as a pit,"
nothing returns from: am I going down the

drain: or am I out still, languid in the long
curvings: (is one not born to delight in the

presence thereof of that which is—or is
spring pollen to bother one): is nothing

sacred: all is: I mean, if a rattlesnake
whirls out of the brushwork and hangs into you

that is terrifyingly sacred: and when
you have wintered with a dark dead rose, the

Scat Scan

springing of the dewy rose is sweetly sacred:
in respect to the sacred, you should get

out of the way of a loose log slipping down the
hill, and watch it when chill turns the rain

slick: if a high wind wrinkles the lake the
sharp-lit ruffles are sacred: and when the

lion snarls and bites in the ecstasy, that is
the glory thereof: nothing, not a single

thing, is secular: but beyond the fact that
everything is sacred nothing whatever is to be

made of it: we do not know whose machinery it
is if it is anyone's: is cum nasty: well,

yes, but there are fire-threads in it that
stitch together life: and what about the mean

old egg: it comes looking: and it kills
thousands for the one it can't refuse, that

won't be refused, the raper of walls and
chemical warfare: alas, the lean cry of the

newborn dik the cheetah squeezes, isn't that
awful: but the cheetah lies down to her

sucklings: the milk that flows is sacred: I
suppose I could go on: it looks as if I could:

Glare

in my last (and nearly first) review from
England, it is observed that I am on automatic,

good lord, is there so little to consider that
it must be reconsidered: throw the abundance

away: wipe it off, shove it over: we are
without limits: except for the little black

bean within us, still in its skin, awaiting
rain: inside that is a darker harder bean:

it is the vitality: it is a hard
bean: it holds the reaching peripheries in

check:

clamp the c (c-clamp?) of clog on log, it's a
dog: is, too: be beep: bittle de doo doo

daw: de daw daw: people always if, if, iffing,
if this, if that, my father used to say

with a cunning air "*if* the dog hadn't
stopped to shit, he'd have cotched the rabbit"

my father when he was being winky-wise liked
to say *cotched*: (my memory is about as long as

your dick: that's fairly short, hiccuped Henry)
no, since you ask, no, I don't write to trim

my way into your approval, though I wish your
approval: and for your censure, it wavers on

the ridge of defining my good: though I don't
care for your censure: still, some things one

doesn't care for are useful, even illuminating
but if I don't let you mess with me, you could

ask why I mess with you: after all, writing
is one thing: allurements to readers, possibly

misleading the worn-out or broke, carry
responsibilities: may you not pay me to do

whatever I please: do you not like to see the
field played, especially played well: (some

writers of traditional verse are better than
others, as are the writers of free verse: it's

not the verse that counts but the difference):
(there really was nothing for me to amount to

except the nothing I am: I mean, by the
smallest amount, sir, by a hair, did I manage

to bring anything off: prospects at my
unfolding were as withered as an old folks'

skin collection: as I grew up things were
said of me by the elders from a

state of half amusement: I was not thought
likely, never likable: look you now who

stuffs bucks and smiles: I say, we are blind
to what we do will do: I say, responsible for

what we intend, what did we intend: help us
out there: do us a little good: I say to

people twisting in their minds, come on over
here to me, honey, I've been twisted fo-fi

times: I know the way to go easy on yourselves:
it was a dark road to find but I lit it up:

you are not the big cheese here: you didn't
set this up: goodness turns out bad, meanness

saves: how are you supposed to know, when you
consider that millions of others are intervening

where the thread will frazzle: but then, of
course, as it were, press the c (as in

c-clamp) in clamp up against lamp and you
have damp: cool.

these cold days in May give me the woolly-willies:
it's hard to maintain an erection out in the

windchill: the young women cannot see your ardent
carriage increased when the wind outlines

them in savory ways: (it takes old guys half
an hour to start pissing and the rest of the

day to finish): southwetserly: why is it that
the truth is not half as believable as the

unlikely: why?, why because the truth runs
from indifferent to terrifying ("we die")

whereas the unlikeliest possibility we have
any evidence of is that ("we don't"): but it

is just the unlikeliness that introduces the
presence of the marvelous, abrogations and

effects only gods could arrange: the unbelievable
(through faith) becomes the most believable

while the dull flood of pure truth, abundant,
overwhelming, obvious, just washes us away:

what has an old man to do with a purpose: what
long field or range of hills has he to play his

purpose through: alas, at the butt end of what
was, he totes up his tedious results and sorts

about in them for a flicker of stone or gleam
of dust, his purpose to reckon up so much

trash played out into dribbles and feints: but
sometimes old men limping about as if on

broken bones will have excellent hearing and
the snickers of the young, or just the rude

impatience, will smite and jar them and drive
them off ever so castaway to the park benches

of neglect and shame: to the young the finicky
faults of the old are comedies split with

contrast: but the butt end of all your days &
ways is a little arousing, if you get my point:

see also, fag end: caught up in the woodsy
wiles, flickers and gleams, of LIFE, Robert,

perceiving he could go either way, went the way
his imagination less frequently went, which

was, for him, the way most people go, so he had
a fairly normal life—house, children, wife,

cow, and a side of poems:

your insidious eloquence makes me seek the
plain dealing of the woods, the dark, the clear

stars: and your refinement, a line so thinly
held I can't tell which side will break from

snide tittering into howling mockery: (a little
extra humidity over, say, recent days has

turned the streets into rivers, embankments
into rubble, and this morning it all turned

into snow—the pink tulip trees luminous
under their clusters of white; the crabapple

blossoms, though, ready to radiate, frozen
out of their sockets, could be, and everywhere

gushy mush cushions the walkways: it is, of
course, Mother's Day, May 11, a good day for

corsages' metallic glaze and fern lace: my
mother is dead and gone, a death 46 years old,

but a death as close as the next cell of my
brain: when in distress with her young brood,

as many dying as living, she cried out "give
me the roses while I live" I had no roses

and the distress taken up into myself, I had
the impoverishment of hysteria, my mouth at

times as I bent over leaking like a fountain,
my dreams full of stiff figures that tried to

move: now that I have whatever I want, coin
or flower, I can give nothing back, the

lips cannot find a smile, the hands cannot
ease into the lap, the eyes cannot light with

calm): how does the magician, who makes reality
vanish, feel when his infected thumb throbs

and a pink streak or two times its way up his
arm: does the magic vanish like an imp

shrieking with mischievous delight: I say,
does the magic of reality take revenge:

well, so it is with the weavers of language
and their cunning cloths that string out of

vestments or take the material out of presences
some day these weavers will be the object of

their practices, and the present will present
them with no present of escape: tell true:

speak plain: deal openly: shed deceit:
these yield no room to the coming round of the

other side: TWO THOUSAND YEARS OF TRASH

truth persists, if at all, hardly distinguishable
from a pack of lies: the truth has about as

much chance as a slender of wheat in weeds:
but, of course, weeds are the truth, too, just

not the truth we want to keep: not that what
we don't want to keep isn't also often true:

for example, some of us, those below the line,
want to think that all men are equal, since

that would raise us: while to others, if all
men are equal, equality would step them down:

well, the truth is that all men are equal, but
you know how it is, you hem and haw, give and

take, squirm and squat, and it all comes out
how you're as equal or unequal as you can

make it: allowances like woolly ramifications
surround these ideal axises (axes?): the

breaking down of things promotes possibility:
as with love, the lucky cannot, except by

scraps and fidgets, hold onto love, while those
who love to the sour bottom of desperation

can let nothing, not even themselves, alone to
live but must cleave to the passion till it

kills, either inwardly or outwardly: thank
goodness for the half assed and easygoing, for

the good stuff from time to time that takes
love on and lets it go: thank the lord for

those who get off in the morning to the office
and clear their minds for stratagem and strife:

we should always believe the opposite of what
is believed because what is believed hides

by contradicting what we don't want to believe:
the truth covers the merely true and the truly

believed. . . .

HASTEN ALONG

the rot of some deep-wasting roots pops bulbs
of white mushrooms up which boil the soil, I

mean, moil the soil (a bile phrase), how, what
a misgo (alack, my best bad writing)—no, no,

my characters aren't characters but charact'ry
all kinds of things played out poorly:

if the temperature, as they say it might, goes
to 25 tonight, the begonias will be gone, the

daffodils will be daffy, and the crabapples
will be, well, crabby, and, of course, the

succulent mother-of-pearl will suck: (sonority
cannot draw the height of his arc but blubbers

underwater like a drowning humpback: these
days: and a man, a writer, said of a man,

a literary agent, that he, the literary agent,
said he liked only gaspable stories: graspable

I said, you mean: no, he, the writer, said:
he said that he, the literary agent, said he

would seek to place only the gaspable: alas,
that ever the age had come to such: but, on

the other hand, dull, bad writing will not hue
up the cry, I whoreson daresay:) there is a

galaxy lies askant the tree-level that spins
its frail arms out to the Hubble lens, and

light traveling at over 180,000 miles per
second can get there in 600,000,000 years: you

can put that in your pipe and smoke it, poof
you're gone: (when you get old you're more

interested in a redistribution of weight than
wealth: the pot lumps smooth with convexity,

the abs lose their trained ruffles, and the
flesh-flabby dugs dangle down: a mispleasaunce

at the end of the road: I hope my literature,
which was mere allusion, has pleased you: I'm

signing off for today, I have to brush my teeth
and get some sleep: tomorrow I have to get

the garbage out by the road by 8 A.M.: (had he
taken the "wrong" road he would have hit an

EVEN BIGGER DIFFERENCE

it is hilarious how sad the world is: I mean,
for us: the planet itself, of course, rolls

on free crushing over our surmises and tribulations:
what is sad is sad but also the silverest

ruffle in the dark-headed storm tower fleets
so fast we burst in tears: we can't tell

whether to look to this moment or the next;
whether to try to hold still while we gut the

moment of its quickest physics, our work as
patient and busy as dungrollers, or to rush off

smartly to possibility in the next tick, a
second chance, perhaps, or another moment just

run over and left: that the world is so bad
off (for us, I mean) is tragic, but the tragic

fully ballooned and fleshed out splits into
peals of tearful aches—I mean, how far can

you go with a funeral before you die laughing:
this defensive device has been as it were

created by the earth for us, an earth that
doesn't care a hoot for a holler: (or

sometimes, from the last minute gold in the
west you can look across to the other side

where a sunken thunderhead is topped in rose:)
desire is an industrial-strength cleanser: no

matter the microbe-ridged crevices of smegma,
the tongues of some will swirl the velvety

precincts of the little bead or some will
slurp as if the clabber of paradise lumps of

cum: glory nestles into a little dirt, and
dirt slickens as fine as ecstasy: well, I

suppose some polar opposite is spread apart
there to arrange the coming together of things

OH, DEAR

you think if you say you're going to die, you
won't die: oh, no, you say, I'm going to die,

you're going to die, we're all going to die:
you think that takes the spell in and

throws it back: la, la, it's like one hell of
a party: but, of course, if we do really get

a party out of it now! but then, how are we
to handle these thorny problems except with

gloves, sprays, and rugged protective devices:
we do not know as much as you might think:

the planets were once all points of light and now
they are so different no crazy inventor could

have invented them: anything looked at
closely becomes wonderful, especially—there

she goes, that flimsy skirt, those legs,
clicking down the hall to the restroom to

piddle that pussy, lord, have mercy, (if
she doesn't piddle her pants getting there): of

all the resources from dark origins, what we
most implore is endowment, to stand in the

fresh embarrassment of involuntary arising
before eager astonishment and juicy possibility,

Scat Scan

to cause terror to tighten bliss across the
sweep of the trembling abyss

    I have nowhere
    to
    go and all
    day
    to get there

trust no one: there is not a shred of loyalty
that will not yield to advantage or change of

circumstance: when you do what you're supposed
to do and others do what they're supposed to

do, trust is not called for: (the point,
actually, is to foray for aye—and not to

yield): (you know how wide the universe is;
we can blow off a few spots and nothing

ever missing): oh, foller the dollar, it knows
the way: dam the way up, so the dollars get

out of hand in mounds, deep chests, and long
keepings, moldy trusts: put your dollars to

work: and stay home yourself: if you don't
have two dollars, start with one: pretty soon

you'll be sitting around thinking of all the
things money can't buy: (it is important to

note that all states are miserable: the only
joy is in thinking it desirable to get from

one to the other, state, I mean: California
is the best state, because you can't get to

another state that way, so your misery can
turn into the delights of imagining an East:

oh, the tricky land of the luck-strewn East,
the painted temples scribbled and scrolled

so amply as to allow the falling out of the
farthest personal chance, number: let's see:

what other moralizing can I do, orders give,
prayers urge—all unimaged, unexampled:

(take Long San Temple, for example, the
dolphins yin and yang circling the center,

a floridity of dragons (florality?) entertwining
the outside of the circle, the inside of the

octagon): Shakespeare, heightening artifice,
renaturalizes nature. . . .

a hip pain, a swollen gum, eyes that stick dry
at night, an ingrown toenail, a skin blemish

precancerous, I tell you, I feel like shoot,
I feel like wasted space: I mean I feel as

out of place as if Mary Scots had feared getting
salmonella from the chopping block: I feel

like deeply undecided old men, drawn backward
more than they can push forward, their

lightning fork-shorn, their little slug soft as
a snail, patches of decay festering in their

groins: I feel approximately like that: also,
I don't feel good: instead of a young squirt

you have a little bulging blubber: I need
help: but you can bet a circumloca(cu)tion

around your asshole (round trip, rim trip) that
when the dogooders get out there saving lives

(don't eat, don't smoke, don't drink, don't sit
around) they're fooling themselves out of

knowing that too many live already (so
hard to accept) and too many live too long

Scat Scan

(Medicare, Medicaid): we save only to drown
in ourselves: not to rush out to save is to

admit the truth: I can't wait for somebody to
save me: when I was ten about I was called up

to the altar of the Pentecostal Fire-Baptized
Holiness Church to be saved and later as I

sat on a bench recovering, an old woman asked
carefully and earnestly if I was saved: hell,

yes, I think: saved from all that froth: no
bit of foolishness people will not take

seriously and the more removed from probability
the less likely it need ever be tested by

reality, so the more deliciously constant, the
purer: I never can quite get over this

propensity, the obviously true forsaken in
search of a delusion in a corny grotto: the

thing for which there is no evidence shines
what only deity knows: that light can intercede

with the worst real circumstance: the people
while foolish are no fools: they go for the

good stuff where it's best obtained, and
cheapest: the gism never fails that is beyond

this world, can't be analyzed into failure:
the fault that can't be mended is no fault:

BLADDER PROBLEMS

you've probably heard the one about the lay of
the land: then there's the one about my

elevator not going all the way to the top
anymore: and, of course, I'm like black

raspberry jam—seedless (actually, I have
plenty of seed, it's germination that's the

bust): but hang, oh, hang, hang on, the fat
lady is still primping in the dressing room: we

have time to consider the considerations,
whatever they were, I've forgotten: what *was*

it all about: oh, yes, it's all about what I
saw this morning as I was sitting in the car

over in Geneva waiting for Phyllis to come out
of the Hanging Gardens store with her hanging

tuberous begonia when coming towards me in the
parking lot was this boy and semi-scraggly

girl and he was trying to press down this
erection, sometimes running his hand in his

pocket: her hair was hanging down and she was
talking: he probably had thought of the tip

of her nipple or the lip of her barge-swinger,
and there he was, ready: that, I said to

Glare

myself, is what I can nearly remember: just
think of gliding, think of that footloose,

fancy-free gliding back and forth between the
stars, and then that stillness you can't hold

anymore than you could hold a tiger, just a
shiver of motion and you are powerfully done

and undone: but it's Memorial Day and those
are memories: some of the people I was in the

war with didn't come back: that is very sad

consciousness is a kind of planet, inscribed
on the outside with whatever's seen or done,

trekked or swum, climbed or scrambled down,
while inside the molten moves (drives, slow

shifts) redispose how the surface lies: we're
wardens, gardeners, waterworkers of the self

keeping the circulations clear and the light
bright; except, of course, we clog everything

up and dumb everything down dim:

     I sit alone back to the window
     in a square of winter sun:
     the curve of the earth
     sinking into the deep beyond
     falls away all around me:
     nothing holds us up but
     a centering in motion, the great
     sun, unpropped, its center being
     hauled off, too,
     motion finding its ties
     with greater clusters and
     centers enveloping

what's up?
what's up?
what's up?
what?
what?

I don't actually like the smell of pricks, I
think: even pussy puts me off if I'm not up

for it: light jam, though, though sticky, a
dab, say, the thinnest apple, can improve the

layout: or a spray, a touch of perfume by the
cheek or lip can really brighten things: art,

so transforming, addresses an aspect or two
but often overrides nature too much, so that

one can long to be back at the beginning, the
substance put forward unaltered in its own

surprise: work with it: who knows what
combinations will do the trick: (listen,

desire can turn the slickest scum marsh
into golden shores): I've

gotten to where no one is included in my
sexual preference: true desire savors its

satisfactions in silence, feels in awe the
piercing surgeries of unforgivable beauty,

stricken heart, pulled gut suffered dumb:
true desire, covert, will not want its eye to

be seen about, because it "takes two," and
meetings glance off killingly as much as tie

together rope to rope: some loudmouth
rattletrap old creep or some feinter and

disguiser will keep the air full of sexual
this and innuendo that, they burst the tension

out of silence, these vulgarians, what are they
about who are about nothing: desire keeps,

rejoices in, and suffers its time: a woman
in her reticences can be deeper than the stars

and twice as foreign: delicacy and harsh
sweetness fill the barge of pain; honor and

service willingly show upon the lips of tender
feeling: the coarse, ah, the coarse, unhappily

they are not refined: to one aright, the
garden of the woman is full of flowers: the

porcelain gardenias of the upper arm, oh, the
marigolds of the armpits, petunias in the

groove between the jaw and neck, oh, the navel
dandelions, oh, the verbena, viburnum, tiger

lilies, musk roses, the orchids of the eyelids
oh, yes, the scent, every inch another, and

every one a seeping nectar, a dew distilled, a pop
sicle: of course, if you get old, sour, and

wrinkled, too stiff to lope, slap, and yodel,
why, then you have to love the spirit more:

by then the flowers have fruited and the
nectarines lie about and the grapes split of

their own plenty, and the casks of honey clear,
and wine, cool as the hecatombs, revives the

flowers of the mind: say goodnight, Archie

GOODNIGHT, ARCHIE

LOVE POEM

1

You can't fill
a shallow
dish

with a strong
faucet:
a

dribble, though,
will brim it
over

2

A baby wren
can't
use

a whole squirrel
but a skinny
flow

of the lacywinged
will soon set
it off

3

You come on
like a comber
foaming

Glare

at the crest:
stir me
only

please as a
pond lap
slips

OLD AGE

Whatever is
wrong

won't

be
wrong long.

this is the beginning of my next piece: I
don't yet know what it's about but I suppose

it's about not knowing what it's about: a
better beginning, however, might have been to

begin before the beginning with a great idea
full of precious content: content may, though,

sometimes interfere with the essential motions
that spell out stuff better than sense does:

essential motion for the most part implies
form, for essentiality is curiously both

highly defined and indefinable: what an
interesting combination: and what kind of

world are you in that you're ending up in: I'd
say, whatever there is an inside to, I'm

outside: up to here I wrote the other day when
a videotaper aimed at me and my old typewriter

and said, write: what was I to write, the
imperative without warm-up or compass: you

have to look out when you let a photographer
into your place: they see quick possibilities

that rearrange your furniture, pull your
window plant out of its disposition to the

light, and work in angles not suggested by the
flat floor and straight wall: my philodendron

has lost half a lobe on a leaf and, for some
reason, the standing lamp won't turn on: I

think poets should keep the doors to their
little work studies closed and seek publicity

in bars and at charity balls, auctions, and
street fights: outdoorspersons: it is not

worth 43¢ to be known as a poet: gangsters
have more fun, partly as a consequence of being

in a low tax bracket: poets would consider it
an honor to get within the range of paying

taxes, whereas gangsters fire back: but honor
is a stale thing that makes you feel stuffy:

imagine getting honor and stiff taxes

my father-in-heaven is my father: my father is
in heaven: that is where nothing, not even my

father, is: there, there is no pain, no strain,
no gain, no train, no rain: so little is there

not even any knowledge of the little is: but,
beautifully, it lasts forever: wherever

anything is it can't stay: but nothing, which
is like the spirit with no body, endureth

forever: this is a hard thought: if this
universe closes down, will anything be missing:

the childlike question, what was here before
the universe was, becomes in time sensibly,

where do I get the forms to fill out to apply
for this job: is it true that if I had never

existed, been born, my existence would never
have existed in the universe: you mean, there

are all these millions of beings that have
never come into the universe and, now, never

will: well, then, is the universe only that
which has come into existence: and would the

universe be different if it had happened
differently: my sisters and I were in the

kitchen one day—the old kitchen, before the
new one was built (on the other end of the house)—

and we were dancing and singing and speaking
in tongues like the big old women at Sunday

meeting, when my mother came in and told us
that mocking the Holy Ghost was an unpardonable

sin: well, but what a bad thing to know, then
I mean: and if you've already done one it

apparently doesn't matter if you don't stop:
we might as well have been let go, never to

know we'd sinned: I was a little boy: I
couldn't lift heavy weights: I wanted some

more unpardonable sins: it seemed like you
could move around in a bunch of them, but what

if there was only one, and it was changeless:
long-lasting intensifications can breed from

some things: my father, too, he squelched
my sass, flailed my anger (whipped my ass):

he dis-tamed me: oh, I been wild a lot: the
title of my autobiography is *Me All Over*:

this isn't it: I have miles to sleep before
I go

     YOU BET YOU BIT

whatever happens now (let's pray that it will
all be, though it is not likely to be, good)

I guess in my 71st year I've had my turn: turn
as in going from something fresh and new to

something old and fresh, no, I mean, old and
stale: or it could be called a turn through

time, a hand sweeping the arc from dawn to
noon to dusk: this familiar poeticism sounds

okay, but wouldn't it be funny if you could
glance up at the sky and see where the hand of

your time was: the sweep for some would be on
a grander scale than for others, which implies

that each of us has his own sky really, some
little bubbles, some crashed hands hanging there

stupidly in the dome, the arc, hardly begun,
incomplete: whereas, some old fogies

dwell with the setting sun and dance in the
dusk like bouncing bubbles, not staying down

and not popping, either: this thing could be
a trope, too, this turn, a spiritual thing,

a thingless thing, a giddy or terrified rise,
even in some cases a comfortable and longed-for

coming down: the young look up and see so much
time they forget the moving hand and only much

(two much's) later are shocked to see the hand
leaning weightily west: alas, was that

lost time, then: what time is unnoted time:
well, so, like, we found these nestled nuts

in a closet corner, and, like, well, Phyllis
said, we have a mouse: so we did because

there he was the next morning in the trap I set
but so then we were watching Seinfeld when

abruptly *another* mouse, like, darted across
the floor, out upon the floor actually and

back, so, well, like, I set the trap again,
but can you believe after two nights it

remains unsprung: I suppose the mouse smelled
death and ran out the way he came, like, gee,

well, it is dangerous; like, he smelled death
and departed: I want to bubble on the brink

provided the spritz isn't pain:

O HANDS OF TIME

BACK UP

if the world were not commonly perceived to be
ordinary, the marvelous would not be valuably

rare: whereas, if it were perceived to be
marvelous, we'd sit about in trial podsnapperies

waiting for the ordinary to come true: so the
world tilts on many a teeter-totter, for

where's the fun (or scare) of anything level,
still, or equal: I no longer (did I

ever) care what you think: I am so much alone,
you are not here: I am here with the words

that like thistle fuzz float away: only when
the fuzz gets away will the world's weight be

dealt with: you, if you were here, would make
the world heavy, wanting to know how it is it

can go away: when we are gone we will not
want to know anything, yet all will be the

same: an answer is not the same thing as a
mountain falls or rose, but, who knows, maybe

it can be the pathway to the cistern of a
spring or a black-diamond millpond cold in

summer: maybe queries and responses give
circulation to the things that sit still and

be: if the circulations sometimes fail, so do
the boulders—a tilting wind, say, a hill

undermined by a floodwash: I don't like too
much grain in my poetry: airiness and light,

the sweet emptiness of thought, transport me:
concretion staggers the burro, especially on

rocky paths through the mountains, where,
sometimes dusty and sore-footed I climb up on

top of everything and nearly break the poor
thing's back:

GET HELP

the news of the week is not much better than
last week's: as improvisational melodies

come and go at the piano, so the mind breaks
against some configuration and makes off into

netlike effusions, or so brooks register at the
surface a crack in the slate and flow on, the

registration dissolving in the mixed motions:
so much goes away that saved would fill the

world up with fluff: in fact, so much goes
away it's a scientific wonder how anything is

still here: I mean, how does so much of it
find a route back and in what condition does

it arrive and by what appearances and means
did it effect the transition: I, myself, am

not a scientist: I do not even spend much time
gathering evidence, so it's unlikely any likely

hypotheses could jump up out of my mounds: the
fact is that so much goes away but hardly

anything really does: that is what gets me:
how does so much stuff slither in and out or

go round and round, shaping up and shipping
out: well, it gives me the heebie-jeebies but

doesn't really make any difference to me: if
things can phony the golden years up out of

rust, why. . . .

PLAYPRETTY

you could wish you were dead before it's too
late; that is, before the devices arrive with

their doctors or before the complications knot
up into stall: you could wish to slip away in

the cool of a late evening, a daiquiri in one
hand, the other up somebody's thigh—all your

money in CDs, not with the MDs: if you
slip away you are merely gone from our time,

dear, dear, *hour* time, for there is no
time frame out there in eternity you should

swerve away from, too awesome to deal with from
our pitiably short perspectives: oh, no: all

you would be missing out on is a little more
business as usual, not, as you have probably

already noted a widely critical matter: still
a worm can be so tender on a new leaf that

just flicking it away ruins it, and you wouldn't
want to risk anything too early: so, now mind

you, mind me and be still—or very certain:

in time all the stories become the same story:
the energies play out and the hole at the end

contains everything: pour in the guilt, the
hope, the sour mischance, the dream, the adroit

turn: there is room enough: after corruption's
overfilling swells pass through, the everything

of everything distills and the grave mound
gives itself back to the level and all of the

everything escapes like a breath from the
scene unseen: meanwhile, though, joy can

break out anywhere: eyes can fall in the
giving up of giving oneself away or the heart

can throb at the simplicity of taking what is
given, the simplicity and the breaking surf:

oft when the question of saving arises there's
not much left to save: or capacity to save:

might as well let it go, they say: it's for
the best: death when death is not the worst

shows up and hangs its shingle out: deliverance
is exactly not what deliverance is: pound to

pound, quid to quo—evenness, evenness, oh,
it's all even: it comes out as much of this

as that, life having been some sort of
imbalance in our favor: how is it it all goes

away yet it's all here: it must go through an
invisible phase somewhere: it's as if there's

nothing to see in there between the going away
and coming round again, a little slice of

invisibility—or else an opacity, the sum of
too many things to think about

live unknown and when you go little knowledge
goes away: live unknown and little knowledge

dies with you: a little thing closes up like,
say, a rose: a bit of dust floats off a

canyon wall: a glimmer of air changes direction:
a barnacle takes its feathers in: a little

feathery loss, like the whisper of a single
sea oat crushed underfoot: so little to forget

what nearly never was, what came and went
unnoted, the glimmer of a sunny brook on a

rock wall in the wild wood: so little grief,
a kind of nonevent, an absence occupying an

absence, an absence moved out of an absence:
but, in a way, lots of knowledge dies with you:

your knowledge: all that, of course, is
expected to disappear and that loss is hardly

remembered in our memories: a whole world,
which was yours, went, though no one else knew

about it: wonder where it went: well, there
are flighty manifestations—things that might

have happened but didn't and things, such as
your world, that sharing never brought into

existence—that is, into an existence that
could be missed and mourned: but in another

way that existence is no more or less than any
existence, since it all ceases, including the

rememberers: well, well, so, so: in one
time frame different things are in another time

frame the same: an odd uprising: if they had
not melted the earth would be caked with

dinosaur bones, so many bones dropped over so
many millions of years: the relatively few

petrifications pour knowledge into us very
similar to memories: just think: the saurs

lived unknown (to us) but now are known, are
becoming known: they are coming into a new

genesis and evolution similar to a genesis and
evolution: perhaps discoveries will unwind a

tale of us, even if of a few, so strikingly
revelatory that all of us known and unknown

will become largely re-known—our makeup,
our meanings so similar that to tell of one of

us will do for all: even when we try to slip
in and out undetected we can trip and leave

a mark: our wills, wherever we turn them,
seldom come up with satisfactory results,

unless, of course, we expected the worst

these are the longest days, the sixteen-hour
daylights, the quick sleeps, so many hours to

potter away and putter about: the baby robins
are nearly grown, though still aflutter to feed

and the nasturtium bucket swung from a crabapple
branch is round with bloom (but using lots of

water): mock orange snows its way out of a
thicket, and the laurel is so sprung with

flicky rain-soaked bloom, I go out and shake
it dry to prevent a split: of course, the

timber rattlers and other shakes are out, as
well (to erect the classic teeter-totter) as

mangoes, nectarines, avocados, pears, plums,
cantaloupes, strawberries, asparagus, many

items trucked in: what a country: nature—
nice, not nice, neither: both: God's in His

heaven, but not all is right with the world:
the nest's foul, befouled: the planet's

riddled, stink flows down the mighty rivers;
dirty water climbs sores up the children's

legs: the orb, the dulled shiner: we cast it
aside, sucked dry: palpability, palpability,

that is the artists' realm: I'm really not a
palpabilitist: seeing into the nature of the

apple explodes its skin, mystifies the sweet:
I want to see how things work: I want to

stand in awe of origins: oh, I have something
to tell that I thought of yesterday: I apologize

for the loss of immediacy spontaneity might
have stirred: and doubly apologize for the

cement of lugubriousness that hardens around
the reconsidered: (is this hilarious, or

what?): well, I mean, what I was getting at
is the closeness with which some polar opposites

are married: for example, that truth is error:
(isn't that a riot?): for when you select

from reality widely surveyed the appropriate
stuff from which to form an assertion, axiom,

affirmation or other muscled manifestation,
you have left behind so much unformed stuff

that your truth is drowned in inopportuneness:
in other words, the road you is on is too

slender to measure the landscape: truths, though,
can be passing views, as of strange bushes

by the culverts, or horrifying bumps in the
mattress: I should have written this down

yesterday (it works for words, sentences,
objects, decisions, etc.) but I was on the

road to the outrageous dentist: the insight
is trivial enough, but I regret the loss of

the freshness

what will time, if time alone will tell, tell:
will the sound of telling soothe, and will the

substance agree: will shrieks of alarm break
out of the pacifications: or will the sounds

work their way down becalmed: how many times,
round so many rocks, the brook water narrows

and ruffles before it gets away, reaches the
lake's undulant mirror: water then flows

through water, unlike the frail insect, caught
inside, trying at the window to fly through

pane glass: a buzz so moderate it can't be
heard, like the death of a friend on a

snow slope with the fields cracking crisp, ice
ice: and dark coming: a rising wind slitting

sleet up the chasms

when I'm interviewed I tell the wide-open
truth, because if I defend myself, my defense

will become noticeable and that in itself will
open up what I'm defending: so I just answer

the questions spontaneously and without
reservation, and this leaves me soundly

unsounded; I mean, inscrutable: I want to be
inscrutable because there are many things

about me I do not wish to reveal and saying
everything hides them: (an old person in his

dotage, I am likely to attempt only what is
unlikely to be likely, thus losing my

incompetence in the lost cases): we stopped
by the Farmers' Market in Syracuse this

morning, and the front due to arrive from the
Northwest bringing southwest winds, somehow,

hadn't arrived—or was still pushing the cold
front before it—anyway, I didn't have on an

undershirt under my summer shirt, and I was
cold, cold out among the geraniums, radishes

called white lightning, plums, pears, onions,
strawberries (for a week more), but I noticed

the people, mostly short and stocky, and not
pretty, so I concluded that it is not the aim

of humanity (or DNA) to make beautiful people
or they or it would hit the mark more often:

ugly, I mean, in the faces, and ugly bodies—
one woman, I remember so squdged down and fat,

I thought her buttocks and cunt could never come
unglued, and yet I thought one could be

overtaken by a brutal need to get in there and
see what it was like: well, I'll tell you, it

was a big morning: integrity spent, I am
faithful to the changes in me

at a roadstand, in Dryden, or just outside,
where the A-frames sprawl and touch the ground

or nearly do, we stopped to look over the
watermelons, cherries (still brought in), and

the owner, sorting strawberries (the last of
the local season), said to me, do you know

people eat 60,000 tons of food in their
lifetime: what, I said: yeah, he said: right

away, I figured out that would be 120,000,000
pounds: he was going that way, because he

couldn't resist the overripe strawberries he
culled from his spilling hands: he said, you

know who the worst people are stop here: no,
I said: Cadillacs, they steal, they bitch

about the prices, cheapest bastards: you don't
mean it, I say: he looks up to check out my

car, which isn't a Caddy: lots of potted
plants, including some spindly looking,

yellowed clematis, and some shrunk-up fuchias:
a shopper was there with his wife, and he had

a three-inch band on each forearm, and I said
to him, pardon me, sir, I hope you don't mind

if I ask what the arm bands are for: tendonitis
he said, I've had them on for two years:

I have to stop jerking and lifting stuff: &
then a man drove up and parked right in the

middle of the driveway, locking the other cars
on both sides in: he walked right off as if

he had noticed nobody: we shouldn't worry so
much about consciousness as unconsciousness by

the conscious: eczema, noxzema, and psoriasis

NOTHING CAN HOLD UP NOTHING,
IT REALLY CAN

I asked C.A. what she thought about, no, what
she believed in: she said, etiquette: that's

like good conduct and not necessarily some
stilted ceremonialism: but if, as C.A. says,

we just behaved properly many of our social
programs (at taxpayer expense) would be 86'd:

as one, myself, who believes that good conduct
should unwind along the lines of individual

liberty and responsibility (that is, with least
governmental oversight—unnecessary in a polite

world)—computers could collect the taxes, but
if we could get everybody in the world mannerly

we wouldn't even need defense, so what would be
the use of collecting taxes, just idle money,

or money that could be thrown around for people
who don't have any to pick up (not, no taxes

due, that they would really need any): utopia
comes so easy: all people need to do is to do

what I say: put Laotse in bed with Confucius,
that gives you interior impetus with external

shaping: a lovely combination, which boredom
could explode: a combination that would not

Scat Scan

play in Colorado, say: two boys abed: no
taxpayer could come of that: (but human

continuance has succeeded so well that we now
against our wills bend our wills to human

discontinuance; at least, a lessening of the
continuance from flood to brook sliver: but,

of course, we must go on fucking as usual: pity
we cannot fuck ourselves, although we can get

off ourselves: and there are vibrators and
rolling balls: something can be done: but,

forget it, fucking can never be the same:
imagine the earnest seeking at the womb to

keep slender and challenged human existence
going! what thrills, when work and play meet

in a single coming: what are we here for but
to fight for our own, to cherish our own, the

tenderness and warmth: get away: only, now,
now, we have to thin out our own, turning against

our own in order to keep our own: it was not
like this before, before when two million

human souls netted their paths into this
planet to try to stay and thrive: (leetle

Glare

vun, leetle vun, vair you goink now): I think
some years back men killed each other for little

clusters of women, till you would get down to
where you'd have one old man besides in a cave

full of women and young'uns: till, then, you
know, a man can't fight off enemies and animals

and catch animals and women by himself, he goes
out and gets him a littler man he can rule and

gives him a little: and that is how many of
the lowly make out and survive: yes, sir, they

watch their ass and say sir when they sposed
to: I crack my window so carpenter bees can

bore nests in the window wood, but the ivy when
it creeps in under the window turns around &

tries to get out—that's because it will lead
only so far away from the light before it

dies back: hell, I know all about hell, and
the darkness: to know the darkness of the

dark is to know one may not survive it: turn
back to the window: get back out into the

light (but keep a sunscreen handy)—the real
light I was talking about is the rising up to

the glory of the being so full of being it has
closed off all, nearly all?, becoming)

GRACIOUS SAKES

all my life I thought a swig was a little bit,
like a taste, only wet, I mean, liquid, come

to find out it's a whole lot, a big swaller:
dad blame it: I don't know when was the last time

I got anything right:

101

I don't care what becomes of me now, I'm
already become of: the end is clear (and

clearly dark) but getting there can be a rugged
road: so, undifferentiated as the end is, I

suppose I would prefer one road to another,
though they go to the same place, but way leads

on to way and you can't tell which road you're
on at first, they look about the same: ages

and ages from now, if there's any story left
to tell there'll be no telling what the story

is: differences can be important where it's
hard to make out a difference: this is so

philosophical! but I better look out: I
might miss the road (if I don't want to): in

any case, whey leads on to whey and pretty
soon the clabber's all gone: I think I'll take

a stanza break here. . . .

THE BEE MITES ARE A MIGHTY
BIG PROBLEM

if results tell the story, mankind should
reexamine the story: such a bunch of characters,

bad plot: nondevelopmental theme, sensationalistic
incidents: too many people lying around in

the streets: too many undernourished: too
many hurt spiritually: too many slaughtered

in the interest of too much unity: (I could
mount up but I'm headed the other way): my

illusions have worn so thin I can see right
through them

LIVER & LOIN

how dangerous a catchy (or wisdomy) phrase
whose brilliantly insightful narrowness could

blank out, outshining, the multiplicity of a
conditioned caution: alas, while we hunger

for a clear and beaming truth to settle our
perspectives down (a foundation upon which to

base a way of life, religion, or musical theory)
we need even more the muddled doubts of our

seeking: for to know is to be at an end,
whereas to know pretty certainly enables our

doings and leaves a hatch (an escape) open to
possibility: hark, we must get along the best

we can, so we won't find out how to do ourselves
in: for every proverb (many proverbs) an

equal and opposite can be found, thereby
indicating that small truths are okay because

half true: but even small truths operating in
small minds can be largely horrifying: I like

it when I bump up against somebody in the
morning, say at the gas pump, and say, what do

you know, and he says, damn little: little
may be enough to pay for the gas: but some

truths are so apparent, nothing can shade
them out—hard truths like death and

taxes, and separation after separation from
the umbilicus to the loss of all connection

in the grave: well, there's just so much to
say about truth that, the truth is, I'm getting

all mixed up: think of all the unpleasant
personal truths: our eyes are truly not

the way we want them: our ears are too large
or misshapen or insensitive: we are

egregiously well endowed or gravely into
shortfall: our skin is acned or the wrong

shade: the ratio of hip to shoulder is off:
I will have to dedicate a whole piece to truth

someday it is so hard to cover: for now, in haste,
I am fragmentarily (and truly?)

WAY COOL

104

Uncle John was a cap'm at the beach back when
the world was trying to begin: those old days

yes, sir: he could spot a school from the
shore: the rowboat would drop, and the men

would haul net out 150 yards into the breakers and
circle back, pop out of the boat and pulling

on each end of the arc drag in a furrow of
fish yea high and 100 feet long—spots,

mullet, croakers, crabs, whale shit, and stuff
like you never seen: the men, black, would

divvy up the catch (except the cap'm got more)
and sell what they could and as dusk came

fires along the beach would break out as the
men boiled fish in iron pots and roasted

sweet potatoes: talk about good: talk about
a hongry: all this is a strain in my makeup:

quite a strain: Lord, how I wish I had lived
then, for that! mincing words will not do for

the flap of a fish on the wet sand: something
you caught, something to sell: I went to

grammar school and plowed the fucking clods
instead, a serious person, little given to

human life: Uncle John was later sheriff for
sixteen years and owned a whole beach: he was

feeling good one day (white lightning) and
reached into the back seat of his Terraplane &

gave me twenty dollars, me, just twelve years
old and in love with nothing but paper pads &

PENCILS

nature poetry, nature poetry
he's got nature
poetry up piss ass

nature poetry, nature poetry
he's got nature
poetry up piss ass DA deDA

I mean DUM de DUM

music for my opening: overture to my manure
(you're out on the highway of life when

unfinished you end butt up):

no, I mean UP piss ASS

the wealthy need the wealthy: no wonder they
have so many parties (to which the wealthy are

invited): the money weighs as a responsibility
heavy with hauteur and guilt: the fortunate

feel they should fall but fear the pit: in
other words they're like everyone else: except

they're rich: I suppose you would like to
know something about my inner life: well, it

stinks: no, no, I don't mean that, I'm kidding:
what I mean is that I think you would like to

think that my inner life stinks, it is so
comforting to know that other peoples' inner

life also stinks: but no, seriously, I don't
mean that about you at all: don't I know how

compassionate and supportive you can be (altho
that seems to pour forth more readily upon the

lost, forsaken, sick, or disadvantageously
challenged; that is, a situation in which

someone else's inner life stinks more than
your own): well, I confess, my inner life

stinks but only when it isn't gloriously
fragrant: merriment runs along kicking up its

heels down all my tragic streets, although when
I get to the theater district both my stink &

my fragrance seem of the stuff they play inside,
entitled bubbles on the marquees of dreams:

so, look out how you mess with me: I have my
finger on your pulse or in something else: you

have to be careful of transcendentalists: on
one side of their goofiness is carnal misery

and on the other the prettiest high slides
glee ever broke out of: that's the amusement

park just down the riverside from the theater
district: who can ever be sure of anything

and the transcendentalists get up there where
there's (goodness) nothing to be sure of:

anyway, I love you, you know I love you, and I
want your life inner and outer to be doused

with radiance, even if it is really a

STINKEROO

what is the difference between a balanced view
of things and sitting on the fence: well, on

the fence, you could get barbs or spikes up your
delicacy: but the thing is, why did you ask:

are you angry at me and want to addle me with
a conundrum, short-circuit my head with a hard knot:

have you developed insufficient faith in my
prior responses (responses verging on answers)

or are you just a miserable little needler who
can't stand anybody else's happiness: I can

tell you what's on my mind (forget about sex):
I'm roaring in the aisles over these long-face

poets who labor (poetically) over their
country's identities and problems: their

symbols are going to come into control of ale
and "mixing and mingling" (forget about sex)

and they're going to work right through hunger
and desolation, if possible before the funding

runs out, and they're going to liberate the
gods in the slobs, marry the spinsters, and

ward off disease: no, I lost it: you know
what I mean: it's just a riot the way people

take themselves: my ribs burble: my eyes are
washed in the salt of my native land: I suppose

it would be only just to give these people
prizes: a leaden example pacifies the people:

that's the best solution right there, effectuate
the lobotomy: give the people what they need,

no resistance to their fates: no, I don't mean
all this: I just mean, isn't it a sight, all

these horses careening around taking themselves
seriously: guess who gives a hoot: well, I

don't know about your nation, but my nation
would just as soon not be bothered, and I

wouldn't want to bother it, would you

BOOBS HOOT

107

Glenn (inventively—and wittily, as is his
kaffeeklatsch wont) (also quite a singer and

maker of songs) said why not let professors
improve their pay (lessening in buying power

since 1968—see, Schwartz) by selling time
to local commercial interests: apart from

the midclass break that lets kids visit the
facilities, one could have one or more mini

breaks, such as, in addition let me suggest
that you visit Zikakis—good sales, good

service: or, Odysseus, come ashore naked,
bristled with brine salt—and now, have you

tried the Downtown Bagelry: not only would
this supplement the poor professor's wage

but it would put the students, unused to such
in touch with the realities that produce the

funds that universities suck off, no, I mean,
suck from: no tuna salad is to be had sucking

off, I mean, from Odysseus, not that the clear
visions of isles and spooky women and

Scat Scan

attractive monsters don't brace the spirit:
Glenn's fun: also capable of pertinent and

deep thought: we like him, as do others: as
a professor myself I am conversant with the

opinion (now conviction) that anything
formulable enough to be taught is not worth

teaching—is, that is, exhausted, unless it
can be revived: for things are said and

taught only to get beyond themselves: students
must rifle through these forms in order to get

to the uncertainty, blips, and hints that
suggest the what-is-to-found is being approached:

so what does the professor have: merely the
possibility of grace in redrawing the line:

I said to my neighbor, both of us new to old
houses, a tree, apparently on the line, has

leaned partly out of its roots toward your
roof, and it must be taken down, and he said,

whose trees these are I wish I knew: were they
planted by your old owner or mine, and are they

Glare

on the line or not, and who's going to pay for
it: all I could think to say was, it looks

a little like the leaning Tower of Pisa—

GET OUT

the past lifts: the burning aches flow ashen: the
heavy waters fog out of the valleys, & trim

the mountain heights: high winds strike the
heights free of my pangs, become swirls you can

see through, too sheer for mares' tails: but
how much is that mockery in the window: why,

it's my reflection, swimmy, ghostly, wavery, oh
I'm just an old fool in a gilded cage: so, I

go on, and my image flies out of there, not for
sale: as it will fly away someday, without

price: what a joke it was: and is: I took
the planet seriously: can you imagine: I

hear giggles along the outer limbs of the
galaxies and belly laughs in the cores: I

made plans, set goals, to make myself last in
something lasting: you can expect a gullywasher

to take failure away, but I succeeded well
enough in a way, and now I am here by the

going-away and my dizzy little arrogances turn
in an overwash to mud: hark: it is written:

better laugh a little yourself, so you join
the universal chorus: get with it: be

there with the high ride: so, now, am I to
take laughter seriously, or am I to laugh at

laughter: but I didn't set the goals for the
goals: no, I set the goals when not for myself

for you or all of us: only in the very last
instant will you be undone in me, for you are

a carbuncled cask, its chain locks encrusted &
salt-sealed on the bottom of the deepest lagoon:

well, I don't know about that: will the worms
send us back to the chef: will we be too rare

or too tough or overdone or sauceless: I
think not: I think we will be acceptable:

anyhow,

LET'S NOT SPOIL THE TRUTH
WITH BEAUTY
HERE, OKAY

109

It's bad news in the OK corral when the
beautiful wrinkle: the skin loosens and dries,

the lips pucker in waste, the eyes droop
outside as if trying to look in: isn't it

specially hard on the beautiful when the looks
look away and they are left, not with their

beauty and the others, but with neither: is
it better to be ugly and unsolicited all

along: sometimes the ugly in age acquire,
what, attractive patinas gained by loss,

flexible wisdoms, acquaintances with distance,
and furthermore their bodies have not been

ravished and ravaged: reality polishes
character and sometimes ugly oldies

shine with a radiance right out of seasoning:
weathered, the beauty and the ugly look about

the same, except for spirit: the ugly rise
into eager equality, while the beautiful are

ashamed to be seen: this, in time, produces a
different facial expression: also, it is

possible that if you are ugly some beauty,
charmed by the foil, will give himself or

herself to you: also (also, also) the rich
who need nothing often look with envy on those

who get shook up over buying practically
nothing: so (so, so) may the good-looking look

upon us, the ugly or poorly endowed (or just
poor), with mercy—so (so, so) we can have a

ball, too

    EVEN AS THE CANNIBAL DOES

if you're constipated don't rape yourself
from the inside out: don't sit down and put

the impulse right to the test, straining and
pushing, causing bleeding: take a little time

to relax, let the tissues adjust: if you lose
the urge, there will be another, if not right

away, soon: gently treated and not pressed
your action will begin to look forward to itself

rather than shrinking back aghast: but, of
course, this is just a little tip to try: it

isn't the law—but it reminds me that if
everybody kissed my heinie that should, my

asshole would be worn smooth. . . .

LORD HELP

when I heard the learned astonisher, I said
to myself, well, I bedanged, I felt so

unpuzzled and, like a text or bottle of
goodie, 80 or 90% proofed, so I went out and

looked up at the stars and said to them, do
you realize how much we mites have found out

about you from this little dot in space: they
did not respond, you might know, because they

are just stars: (if I killed myself, then I
would only be dead: the achievement, unlike

the gesture, would not be great): I would like,
in spite of this alarm and that enfeeblement,

to hold on: the unfolding is not finished:
the big thing remains to do: but what is it:

is it a cluster of small things, terribly
honest, even if filthy and low-drawing, or is

it, as I always thought it was, the inclines
of the peaks, the coming together, so high

that only the unspeakable shares anything with
it: oh, yes, oh, yes, oh, god, I love the

dibble of the beginning rain, the blue storm
off in a rumbling locus and coming here, the

Scat Scan

wind holding, the humidity high, before the
falling out of the playing through: when

the wind strikes, everything will bend over:
the brunt will break, ease will rise again:

the Lord of the rain is where the swirls make
up and where the synthesis crests along great

sweeping lines of fronts and water appears,
but also there is the primate lord, the big

guy at the top of the order, in whose favor is
ease and place and out of whose favor are the

anxieties of hell, the peripheral body without
a body: order at all costs, because only in

that tent may the infant nurse, the seed set,
the loom waft, for when orders collide (the

cost of order) the wounded and the dead precede
supper's menu:

DON'T ASK ME

in the middle of the piddle there's a puddle:
well, it's Monday morning, and it's business

as usual, no business: because it's summer
and the days are agetting shorter: up on the

north end of the west ridge where the sun sets
you can see, marking it off, it's coming back

this way: when it pales out front behind that limb
of the crabapple tree, nights will be long &

brittle cold: are plus a is area: I am
finally fatally flawed, I daresay: the pain

in my hipjoint and humerus is—well, not very
funny: the swelling in the ankles promises

plenty: and a network of other ailments is
so complicated balancing one ailment

tilts another: medication becomes
virtually self-diseasing: so many pills you

can't tell the effects from the side effects:
and who are you, someone before the medications

or during or after: at least, you are being
kept, but in another place: are your feelings

lofty or zolofty, red or blue, down or double
downdown: do you, in this condition, have any

right to speak, for who or what is speaking, is
it milligrams or anagrams, is it tranquility or

tranquilium: will we psyches be like the
skies: we'll never again see clouds that may

not be vapor trails: we'll never be clear and
know our clouds for what they are: maybe we'll

forget about clouds altogether and just tune
ourselves to blue skies, all of us: where wd

the disheveling fun come from then if we
refused any more wars—think of the sublimity

of civilians in mass graves, some with holes
in their drawers for raping: wd we have no

more heroes, no skinny escapees, nobody to weep
over, no generals accepting the fates of

thousands into their strategies:

    NEVER HAS THE GRASS BEEN
      SO WELL WATERED,
    RAIN WATERED, I MEAN

can one be powerful and not invoke nightmares,
bad family scenes, ugly diseases, or immolation,

can one be kindly and yet movingly present:
must one divulge his drives and practices, and

must they be low and damaging in order to
entertain others: may one not weakly put out

his airy net and catch the butterflies or more
weakly put out some sugar water and let the

butterflies go: was it not suggested by the
ancient ones that the valleys outlive the

peaks and that to yield is to let something
headstrong pass: should one disturb another

with a strong emotion or a psychological twist:
even when the complacent crowd beg for a

forceful focus, a motive that impels a single
way, and even when they offer big money and

wide acclaim, should one assume the office and
make something up: complacency to the

complacent, some would argue: may one, for
those few already rocked by horror and in no

need of vivifying pain, may one, for them, let
the drought brook trickle all day, let the

breeze touch the pond like a thought, so they
may be quieted and strong when the grizzly

walks up: alas: nature's mixed: white
clouds float serenely through a summer afternoon

or fangs fly out of a bush at you: should
poems rehearse the terrors so as to leave us

apprised, and should poems at other times hum
the frantic into a pause: I long for a poem

so high, but not too high, where every agony
can be acknowledged as a quiver in the easy

ongoing of the pacific line: love is a kind of
violence; death takes hold sometimes violently:

grief's gusts nearly break your ribs: we deal as
best we can with these but running through, and

rising, is the constant will that longs for
companionship with an all-keeping indifference

YOU'VE NEVER
SEEN ANYTHING
LIKE IT
OR LIKED
ANYTHING SCENIC

the world, so populous, is so decimated: there
were 40 aunts and uncles: there was Aunt

Blanche, and Uncle Claude, Aunt Mitt, Aunt
Kate (I loved her), Uncle John (commanding)

and Uncle Frank (soused), and Aunt Lottie,
Addie, Laura. . . . I believe I believe; no, I

believe: but in what: I believe in belief:
that's hollow belief, the form of belief, without

substance: does that do any good, do you
think: well, I would say, if I may say so,

that at least you'd be favorably placed in
attitude: I don't know if you ever noticed

it, but what you tell yourself can make a
difference: it cannot, as far as I can tell,

keep, say, the house from burning down, but it
can be useful to say to yourself—so, look,

it's not like it's the end of the world: we'll,
I'll, you'll rebuild, start over: the sun

comes up tomorrow (in all likelihood): it wd
not be useful to say, that's the end of me:

so make all the "good" working internal
differences you can—and there are even

circumstances in which internal difference can
influence external difference: for example,

when the aforementioned grizzly issues rapt
from the bushes, what you do may influence what

he does: I don't know what you should do: I
think I heard you should be still and not

scream: maybe unless he comes at you, then u
should commence to shout and wave your

arms: I'm not sure about that: but if you
keep your head while all about you people aren't

keeping their heads, you may be chosen as their
leader: absotively and posilutely:

> LIFE IS A SUEÑO, ALL RIGHT,
> ALSO A TRIP
> (AND ONE HELL OF A NOTE)

I just can't buy the bi- words: bye, bye to
them and their double meanings: bi-monthly:

is that twice a month or every other month:
what is the matter with "every other": say,

every other week, or fortnightly: what's the
matter with fortnightly, except it sounds like

the Brits, and who can stand the Brits: I
cannot, to pause momentarily, bear the Brits:

the wind in their sails would not blow a gnat
off his podium: they are so flat they slip

under linoleum: they look, frankly, as if
they rarely see a washcloth: and on TV they

sound so gruff, just in saying, good morning,
how are you (if they say that), you think

they're getting to gnaw each other: the Brits
is, by rumour, shits, I mean, twits: what,

bubble lips, do you mean by that, says razor
(no, blade) lips: bubbles and blades, bubbles

and blades: have you ever heard it said you
shouldn't buy shoes in the morning: for

because with day's stress your ankles swell
and what fits freely at dawn racks your

leggings by dusk: of course, if you go out
too late to get fit, the next morning your

sloppy shoes fall off your feet: this may be
an exaggeration, but maybe not: suppose you

are gouty or weak-hearted or hyperhydrated,
this exaggeration may be an understatement:

you may have to swath your ankles in the
morning and disbandage them at eve: rather

than shoe fit foot, in other words, make foot
fit shoe: when the bull elephant, his ears

heisted, takes out after a cow, his biswanger
so long and heavy it loops to the weeds, well,

then you think, does it really need to be that
long: does it need to reach in that far: now,

big surprise! when the cow sulls at last and
he flaps it up there, it's in, and you think,

what a trip for the ole boy down that love
canal: true the trip is over before you can

Glare

pack a lunch, but, heck, how long should a
two-year celebration take, all that dense and rhythmical

commemoration:

BEFORE LONG

some notes: buy morning shoes in the morning
and evening shoes in the evening: okay, so

sure, fill the veins with ore, but let them
be the veins of butterfly wings, lest the fill

sink like pig iron: for it must be remembered
the weightier matters are given to butterflies to

fly away with: pitch the lighter problems to
the pigs, they make a wallowing mud of them,

just as people might lack a substantive medium
without their little worries and remedies:

(this note is turning into a dissertation):
a further note: 'twere foolish to be foolish

and wise to be wise (although, I suppose, it
were sometimes wise to be foolish and foolish

to be wise): one last (or still further) note:
soil sticks thinly to the slated hillsides

around here, and rain, when it rains, and it
sure has rained this spring and summer, along with

even moderate winds, the roots of tall spruce
wobble in their sockets, the grasp so slight,

and the trees lean toward the roofs, a pity,
the electrical wires could come down with the

trees and shingles and timbers could fly: it
is better to rent, except then you never get

your roots down and a little blowoff is all
you could need to move you away: last note:

elephants live a whale of a long time. . . .

OFF AGAIN

what are the structures of upholding: how do
they hold: to what heights do they attach to

point and steady them, and upon what ground can
they settle: will the base rock swim, and the

heights, lo, they burn away in the sun, mists
and fringes of fire: of what material can so

high an arising as we need be made: why, of no
earthly thing but of will, blank will, which

acquires nor wields weight but simply insists
that it is as it is, right through the ruins of

truth which melts to reservation and contradiction
right through the rigors of all loss, no more

nothing than the nothing at the end it joins:
so, let us look about us in spite of what

applies and say what must be: what must be:
you ask: (the crows gathered somewhere across

the hill this morning—August 3—and there
was a flurry of raucous introduction, the new

young, ready to fly, getting acquainted with
the old community, winter together ahead, the

isolations of summer-rearing behind): I try to
hide the old fool playing the fool, but you

hear, don't you, the young man, still young,
still under there saying yes yes to the new

days darkened howsomever: it is a sad song but
it sings and wants to sing on and on and when

it can no more it wants someone else to sing:
to sing is everything but it is also specifically

to dive the stave into marshy passageways and
bring relief and the future singers in. . . .

FLAWS AND DRAWBACKS